# BHARAT 2035:

*The Climate Crisis No One's Talking About*

**Mudit Jain**

**ASTITVA PRAKASHAN**

Parijat Heights, Bilaspur, Chhattisgarh 495001, India

First published by Astitva Prakashan 2025



ISBN: 978-93-7002-774-9

MRP: Rs.270.00



astitva prakashan

# About the Author

Mudit Jain never set out to be an environmentalist. He is an everyday urban Indian, living the fast-paced, screen-heavy life, until a heart-breaking incident last year changed everything. A security guard in his apartment complex collapsed from heatstroke during peak summer. That moment hit harder than any headline ever could.

Instead of scrolling past the tragedy, Mudit took it personally. He installed coolers in his building, began questioning his lifestyle choices, and started digging deeper into the climate emergency knocking on India's doorstep. What he found was terrifying, not just the data, but the silence.

Professionally, Mudit runs Happy & Hungry - The Event Co., a company championing sustainable, eco-conscious events across India and Middle East. But this book isn't about his profession, it's about his personal wake-up call. Bharat 2035: The Climate Crisis No One's Talking About is his way of screaming into the silence, loud, emotional, fact-packed, and brutally honest.

Through this book, Mudit hopes to connect with fellow citizens who feel something is wrong but don't know where to begin. It's not about preaching. It's about pausing, reflecting, and doing something, before it's too late.

## 🎧 Feel the Words, Not Just Read Them

Music has the power to say what words can't.

Scan the code and let 'Bharat 2035 - The Climate Soundtrack' take you deeper into every emotion, every moment.

# Authors Note

*The heat came before the siren.*

June 2024.

It was one of those days where the heat didn't feel like weather anymore - it felt like punishment.

That afternoon, I got the call. The guard at our society - the one who stood 12 hours a day at the gate, the one who always smiled, who took cold water from our home every evening - he was gone.

Heatstroke.

He collapsed outside a chemist while trying to buy an ORS packet. No ambulance arrived in time. The road was melting. So was the system.

He wasn't a climate statistic. He was a human being - one of the first silent casualties of a war we refuse to name.

That day, something changed in me. I installed water coolers in the society. It felt good - for a week.

But the discomfort didn't leave me. Because I realized… this wasn't a freak tragedy.

This was a trailer.

And I had seen the full film. In headlines. In hospitals. In the taste of the water. In the colour of the sky.

The climate crisis in India isn't coming.

It's already here.

But here's the catch: Most people don't know it's the climate. They think:

- It's just another bad monsoon
- Just another Delhi smog
- Just another dead river
- Just another heatwave that will pass

But they're wrong.

These are not separate events. They're symptoms of a system that's falling apart - quietly, quickly, and in plain sight.

This book isn't a research paper. It's not a policy brief. It's not a political rant.

It's a warning. A confession. A mirror. A map.

It's based on facts, yes - every number in this book is sourced, grounded, and real.

But it's also filled with stories. Stories of people who lost, people who fought, and people who are still figuring out how to breathe, drink, and live in a world that's becoming unlivable.

And if you're holding this book, I hope you're ready.

Because once you read what's inside - you can't unsee it.

The year is 2035. And this is the climate crisis no one's talking about.

Until now.

# Contents

## Part I: The Crisis We Ignored



## Part II: The Comeback Begins

# Part I

## *The Crisis We Ignored*

# Chapter 1

# The Silent Storm

*It's already happening. You just haven't connected the dots yet.*

**June 2024. Noida.**

The afternoon sun was brutal.

Not the "just hot" kind of brutal.

The kind that claws at your skin.

The kind that blurs your vision.

The kind that kills.

The security guard in our residential society had been on duty since morning. He wasn't new to this weather - North India's summers are notorious. But this year was different. The heat wasn't just uncomfortable - it was suffocating.

At around 2:30 PM, he collapsed.

By the time help came, it was too late. Death by heatstroke. No, not in a remote village. Not in the desert. In the middle of an urban residential colony. Just a few meters from air-conditioned apartments and chilled RO water tanks.

This wasn't an isolated incident.

## India Is Boiling

According to the India Meteorological Department (IMD), the summer of 2023 saw record-breaking temperatures in over 15 states. Delhi crossed 49.2°C, the highest ever recorded in the city's history.

In the same year, over 3,000 cases of heatstroke were reported across the country. 241 people officially died from heat-related illnesses — and that's just what was reported. Experts believe the real number could be 3 to 5 times higher due to underreporting and misdiagnosis.

But here's the scariest part:

Heatwaves in India have increased by over 200% in the past 50 years. And they're now starting earlier — sometimes even in March.

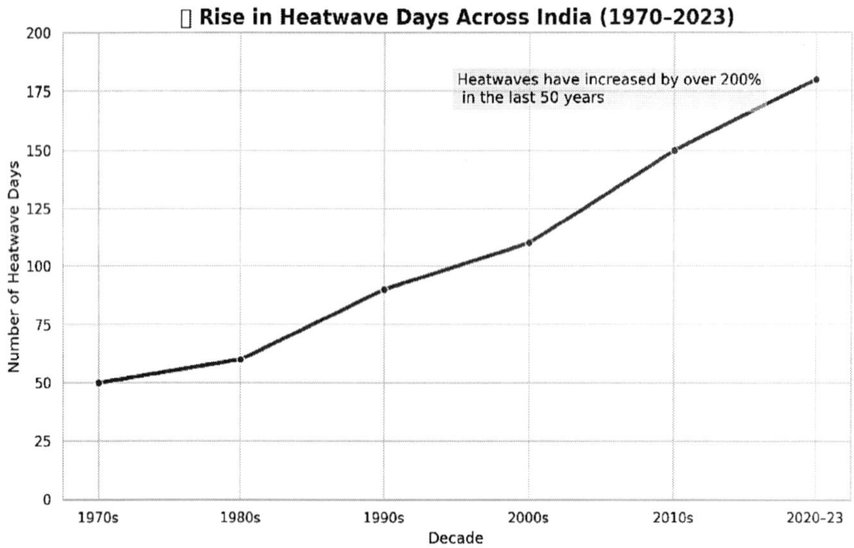

## Urban Heat Islands: Cities That Cook You Alive

Ever walked on a tar road at noon and felt like your shoes might melt?
That's not just imagination — it's science.

Indian cities like Delhi, Bengaluru, Chennai, and Hyderabad have become urban heat islands. Concrete buildings, paved roads, and the vanishing of trees trap heat and make city temperatures 3°C to 7°C higher than nearby rural areas.

Let that sink in — You could step out of Gurgaon into a nearby village and feel cooler air, just because the soil is still there, and the trees haven't been ripped out.

We turned our cities into ovens. And now, they're baking us alive.

## Who Suffers First? The Ones We Never See.

The guard who died wasn't wearing a cooling vest. He didn't have access to electrolyte water or fans. He didn't have the luxury to stay indoors.

India's gig economy - delivery workers, guards, vegetable vendors, e-rickshaw drivers - are now front-line victims of climate change. They're not dying slowly in the future. They're dying now.

## But Why Aren't We Panicking Yet?

Because we've normalised it.

We say,

"It's just a hot day."

"We used to play in the sun, what's the big deal?"

"AC laga lo yaar."

But the truth is this:

We've forgotten what normal feels like.

This isn't just summer. This is a warning.

A symptom of a much larger storm building up.

## What 2035 Might Look Like (If We Don't Act Now)

- Temperatures could regularly cross 50°C in major Indian cities.
- Heat-related deaths could triple, becoming one of the leading causes of mortality.
- Outdoor work hours may drop drastically - crippling India's economy and informal labor force.
- Electricity grids will collapse more often due to cooling demand - pushing the poor into dark, airless rooms while malls and towers stay li

## A Wake-Up Call

That guard's death was a tragedy. But it was also a mirror. One that shows what happens when we let our environment collapse quietly - while we scroll, sip iced coffees, and blame the sun.

This is not "climate change" happening in Antarctica or some sinking island on National Geographic. This is Bharat - sweating, burning, collapsing.

And this is just the beginning.

## Coming Up Next:

Chapter 2: Choked Lungs, Choked Cities Inside

The invisible killer that's already inside your home — air pollution, the quiet genocide of Indian metros.

# Chapter 2

# Choked Lungs, Choked Cities

*You may not smell it. You may not see it. But you're breathing it every second.*

It starts with a cough.

Dry. Persistent. You ignore it.

Then your child begins sneezing every morning. Your mother says her asthma's getting worse. You wake up with a heavy head and itchy eyes. And yet you tell yourself, "It's just the season."

No. It's not the season. It's the air.

## The Day Delhi Disappeared

November 2023, Delhi.

Air Quality Index (AQI): 512. That's not "very unhealthy." That's "hazardous." To put that into perspective, a safe AQI is under 50. Delhi's was 10 times worse.

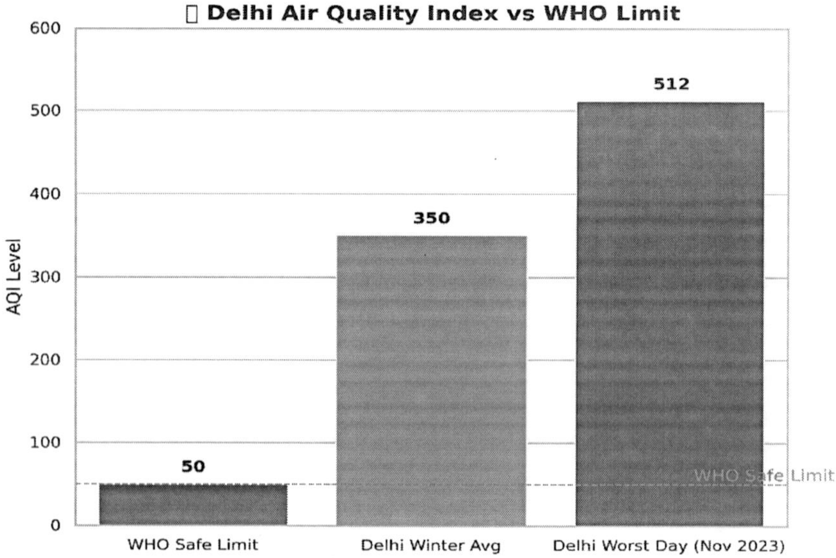


That morning, thousands of flights were delayed. Schools were shut down. Construction was banned. But here's the thing: people still had to go to work. Delivery boys still had to ride. Cab drivers still had to drive. Guards still had to breathe.

You couldn't see Connaught Place from 100 metres away. It was like the city had disappeared in its own poison.

## Welcome to the World's Most Polluted Cities

Out of the top 20 most polluted cities in the world in 2023, 13 were in India.

These include:

- Delhi
- Ghaziabad
- Noida

- Bhiwadi
- Hisar
- Kanpur
- Lucknow

And it's not just the metros. Tier-2 cities are worse off because they don't have the visibility or infrastructure to even monitor their air quality properly.

## What Happens When You Inhale India

Here's what air pollution is doing to your body – today, right now, silently:

- It's shrinking your lungs.
- It's increasing your risk of stroke and heart disease.
- It's leading to early-onset diabetes and infertility.
- It's causing low birth weight, delayed brain development, and even autism in children.

A 2020 study published in *The Lancet* showed 1.67 million deaths in India were linked to air pollution in a single year. That's over 4,500 deaths a day. Every. Single. Day.

You're more likely to die from breathing in India than from any infectious disease.

## Real People. Real Suffering.

Sakshi, 27, a software engineer in Gurgaon, started having trouble breathing during her morning walks. Within two months, she was diagnosed with chronic bronchitis. No, she never smoked. But she lived in Sector 57 – just 500 meters from a burning garbage dump and an unregulated diesel generator zone.

Ravi, 9 years old, in East Delhi, now uses an inhaler every day. His school is next to a traffic-clogged flyover where diesel fumes are constant. His doctors call him one of India's "climate children" — born into a world that's poisoning him from day one.

## Where Is All This Pollution Coming From?

You'd think it's just Diwali crackers or crop burning. That's a small part of the truth.

The real daily culprits are:

- Vehicular emissions (especially diesel and two-wheelers)
- Construction dust (India's urban sprawl is constant)
- Road dust (potholes, broken pavements, uncleaned streets)
- Garbage burning (millions of tonnes of unsegregated waste)
- Unregulated industries and backup generators

Ironically, the people who create the least pollution — our sanitation workers, domestic help, gig workers — suffer its effects the most.

## Children Are the First to fall

India has over 120 million children under the age of 10. And they are breathing twice the pollutants adults do, because:

- They breathe faster
- Their lungs are still developing
- They're shorter — and closer to tailpipes and dust

In Delhi, children have been found to have lungs of a 60-year-old smoker. By the time they reach adulthood, many of them will already be on medication for life.

## The Cost of Ignoring It

- India loses over $150 billion annually in productivity due to pollution-related diseases.
- Students score lower in memory and comprehension tests on high-pollution days.
- The real estate value in some areas of Delhi-NCR is dropping because of unlivable air.

And yet, there's no outrage. Because it's silent. It's not dramatic. It doesn't scream. It just kills you slowly.

## The Invisible Killer

Imagine this: If 4,500 people were dying every day from a visible terror attack, wouldn't the nation be in chaos?

But when it's the air, when it's everywhere, when no one's blamed — we adjust. We accept. We die quietly.

This is not "bad air." This is chemical warfare on the middle class.

## Coming Up Next:

Chapter 3 : When the Taps Run Dry

We feared polluted air, but forgot the threat of disappearing water.

From overflowing bottles to bone-dry pipelines, India's water story is spiraling fast.

Next, we trace how even the most privileged cities are running out of the most basic resource: water.

# Chapter 3

# When the Taps Run Dry

*No war begins with a gunshot - some begin with a bucket*

The scariest thing about a crisis is not when it explodes — but when it quietly disappears from the tap.

You wake up. Walk to the kitchen. Turn the tap.

Nothing.

You open the bathroom faucet. It coughs, then wheezes, then dies.

No water.

Not in a remote village. Not in a desert state.

In your ₹1.2 crore apartment. In a metro city. In a society that boasts of luxury amenities but now begs for tankers.

Welcome to urban India's most ignored emergency — the great vanishing of water.

## The Myth That Cities Are Water-Secure

For decades, we thought the water problem was *out there* — in drought-hit villages, barren farms, dusty wells.

But now, it's here:

- Bengaluru ran dry in March 2024. Tankers were booked out. People fought over borewell schedules.

- Chennai turned off public taps in 2019. IT companies asked employees to work from home due to water scarcity.
- Delhi NCR residents buy water at ₹2,000 a tanker during peak summer.
- Hyderabad and Pune saw water restrictions in multiple housing societies — even as malls and hotels kept operating.

This isn't just a dry spell. It's a design failure. A disaster we built

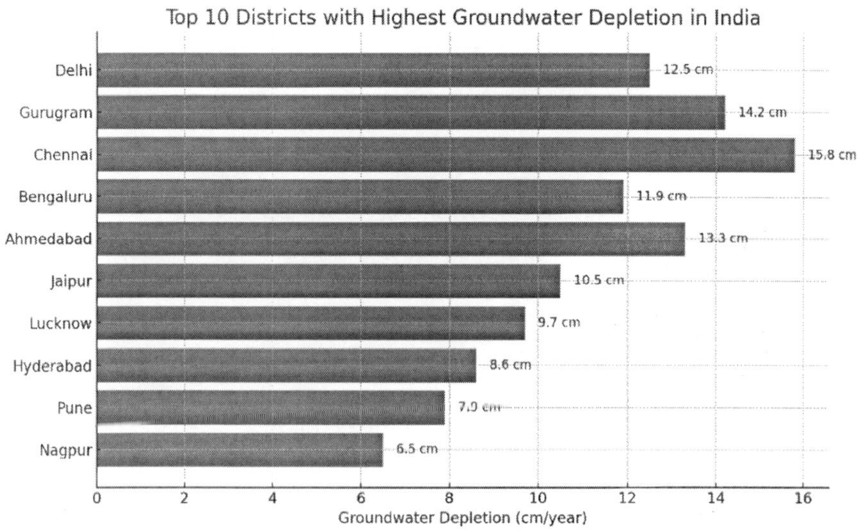


- and watered every day with our carelessness.

## How Our Lifestyles Are Killing Water

Let's break the illusion.

Here's how much water we waste without realising it:

- A single 10-minute shower = 100 litres
- RO purifier = wastes 3 litres for every 1 litre consumed
- Washing machine = 60–90 litres per cycle
- Brushing with the tap open = 10–12 litres

- Watering a lawn = up to 400 litres a day
- Washing your car with a pipe = 120–150 litres

In most homes, 60–70% of water is wasted on comfort and convenience. We're not bathing — we're draining.

## The System Was Never Built for This Demand

India's cities have outgrown their water supply networks. Fast.

- Piped water often reaches only 60–70% of urban populations.
- Leaks in old infrastructure waste over 40% of municipal supply.
- Rainwater harvesting? Mostly on paper. Either not installed or not functional.
- Groundwater? Declining at an alarming 1–2 meters per year in many cities.
- Urban lakes and tanks? Encroached, filled, forgotten.

Meanwhile, apartment towers rise - with multiple bathrooms, lush gardens, and swimming pools.

This isn't demand. This is denial.

## The Urban Water Emergency No One Talks About

Every summer now feels like a slow-motion disaster:

- Society notices go out: *"Please limit water use. Tanker delayed."*
- Elevators stop mid-floor due to low overhead tank levels
- Families fill buckets at night "just in case"
- Maids bring their own water or stop coming altogether
- Kids are told: *"Use the bathroom in school - ours is out."*

You don't realise how much your life depends on water - until it disappears for half a day.

Or a whole one.

And when it does, nothing else works - not the kitchen, not the toilet, not your routine, not your dignity.

## Why Didn't We See It Coming?

Because the scarcity didn't arrive with thunder. It came as:

- Shorter supply hours
- A slow decline in tap pressure
- An extra tanker ordered every month
- The society's borewell getting deeper, then dry
- A plumber saying, *"Bas 10 minutes aur chalega pump."*

We ignored the warnings. Because they came disguised as inconvenience - not disaster.

But what we're living now is collapse in slow motion.

## The Silent Class Divide - Even in Water

Let's be clear.

Water is still flowing somewhere - just not equally.

- Posh towers import tankers.
- Slums fill from leaky pipes.
- One household fills a bathtub.
- Another sends their child to the next block with a bucket.

Even in the same city, the difference between *hydrated* and *helpless* is often just a few thousand rupees or your pincode.

That's not a water shortage. That's a failure of priorities.

## Conversations That Have Become Common

"Fill all the bottles before 6 AM."

"Don't flush unless necessary."

"Call the tanker guy again."

"Tell them to skip floor cleaning today."

"Turn off the RO. We're running low."

"Let's shower at the gym."

"Send the kids to nani's house for two days."

These are the real, raw signs of a city in crisis.

Not headlines. Habits.

## Final Warning: The Day You Can't Buy It

Right now, you can still pay for water. But what happens when money isn't enough?

What happens when the groundwater is gone, and no tanker shows up, and the heat touches 50°C, and the society's tanks go empty by noon?

That's not distant.

That's Bharat 2035 - unless we wake up.

Because the truth is:

You can live without fuel.

You can survive without Wi-Fi.

But you cannot last three days without water.

And that's what makes this the most urgent crisis of all.

## Coming Up Next:

Chapter 4: Rain, Rage & Ruin

When the skies don't listen, and our cities flood not because of too much rain - but because we left them no place to breathe.

# Chapter 4

# Rain, Rage & Ruin

*"It didn't flood because it rained. It flooded because we built like it would never rain again."*

It began with a drizzle. You opened Instagram. Someone posted a Story: "Rain, finally!" You smiled. Monsoon had arrived.

An hour later, your phone buzzed: "Water has entered the basement."

Another text:

"Don't take the elevator. It's stuck on B1."

By evening, your power was out. Your car was submerged up to the windshield. The road outside your society looked like a river. And someone on the society WhatsApp group said, "The sewage water is mixing with the drinking line."

## Rainfall or Wrecking Ball?

Every year, across India's major cities - Delhi. Mumbai. Bengaluru. Chennai. Gurugram. Hyderabad - the rain doesn't fall. It attacks.

It seeps into basements, short-circuits transformers, halts metros, and brings billion-dollar cities to their knees.

In Bengaluru (2022), tech parks in Sarjapur and Whitefield were under 3–4 feet of water. Office-goers commuted in tractors. Homes worth ₹1.5 crore had sewage water in kitchens. Luxury cars floated like boats. And startups lost crores — not to market crashes, but to clogged drains and collapsed roads.

## Why Is This Happening So Often?

Here's the hard truth: It's not because we're getting "too much" rain. It's because we've built cities that can't handle the rain they always got — and are now getting even more.

- Drainage systems are outdated, or never built at all
- Concrete covers everything, leaving no place for water to be absorbed
- Lakes and wetlands have been replaced by malls and towers
- Stormwater drains are clogged with plastic and sewage

Nature gave us a sponge. We built on it with tiles.

So when the skies open up — even for 90 minutes — cities go under.

## A City Drowns Differently Based on Your Pin Code

Let's talk inequality.

- In Noida, Sector 150's villas hire water pumps and private flood barriers
- In Mumbai, Bandra's towers drain water into slums
- In Chennai, the poor climb onto tin roofs during floods — while upper floors live-stream the disaster

It's not just climate collapse. It's climate privilege.

## Real Stories. Real Loss

Avinav, 32, lived in a ground-floor apartment in Gurugram's upscale Sector 67. One night in July 2023, his living room flooded. He lost his laptop, fridge, documents - everything. His insurance didn't cover "natural disasters." He now stores valuables on shelves - like a refugee in his own home.

Farooq, 28, a Zomato delivery rider in Bengaluru, was swept off his Activa in a waterlogged underpass. He survived. Barely. The company replaced nothing. He now wades through flooded lanes with food bags held above his head.

Kamla, 60, lives in Mumbai's Dharavi. During the 2023 monsoons, she slept on a cot surrounded by 4 inches of water for 6 straight nights.

This isn't drama. This is reality - repeated every monsoon, worsening every year.

## What We've Lost (That Could've Saved Us)

- Lakes: Bengaluru had 280 lakes in the 1960s. Today, fewer than 70 remain - most encroached or turned into garbage dumps.
- Wetlands: Mumbai has lost over 50% of its wetlands to construction. These were natural shock absorbers for floods.
- Open ground: In Delhi-NCR, over 70% of surfaces are now paved - which means zero absorption, only runoff.

When you cover a sponge with plastic and pour water — what happens? It floods. Always.

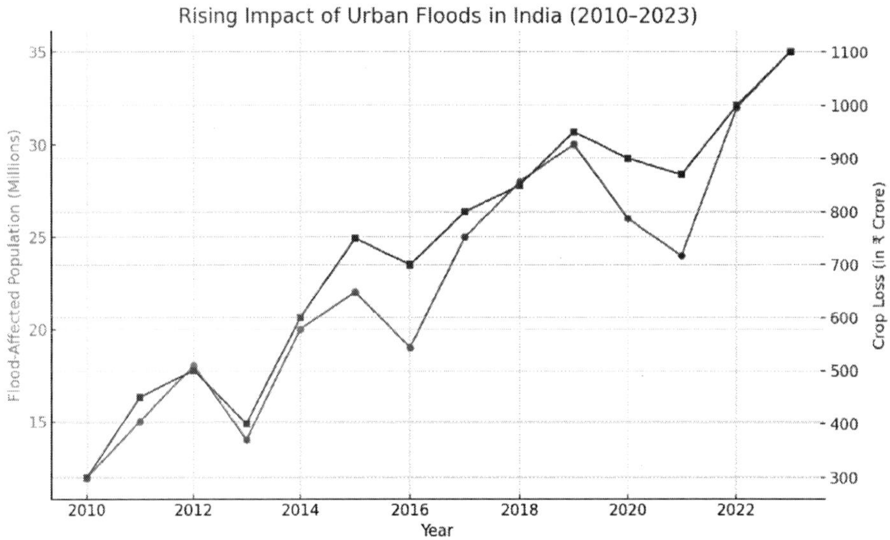


## This Isn't Normal - It's the New Normal

You can no longer say: "Yeh har saal hota hai."

Yes, it happens every year. That's not routine. That's a pattern of destruction.

Climate change means:

- Shorter monsoons with more intense rainfalls
- Storms that dump a month's water in a single day
- Seasons overlapping - rain in January, droughts in August

It's not just unpredictable. It's unmanageable.

## Smart Cities, Dumb Drainage

You know what's truly ironic?

India's urban "smart city" projects boast:

- Surveillance cameras
- WiFi zones

- Digital dashboards

But most of them still:

- Use 100-year-old British-era drains
- Lack separate stormwater and sewage systems
- Have no working flood alert systems

We're trying to go digital… while drowning.

## 2035: The Monsoon Mayhem Ahead

If nothing changes, here's what you'll face:

- Flood alerts as common as weather updates
- Monsoon holidays in schools like we have for heatwaves
- Real estate value collapse in flood-prone zones
- Monsoon migration - where families temporarily move to drier relatives' homes during peak rain
- Health crises - dengue, cholera, leptospirosis outbreaks doubling in urban centres

We're not just battling water. We're battling the consequences of our greed.

## The Rain Isn't Angry - It's Honest

Nature isn't punishing us. It's simply reacting.

We killed our lakes. We buried our wetlands. We built over every last patch of breathing earth. Now, water has nowhere to go - except into our homes, cars, elevators, and lungs.

This isn't a natural disaster. It's a man-made flood.

And 2035 will not be kinder.

## Coming Up Next:

### Chapter 5 : *The Green We Buried*

Before the floods, before the droughts - there were forests.

But in our race to build cities, we buried the very green that once protected us.

Next, we uncover the forgotten truth about India's vanishing forests - and what it's costing us.

# Chapter 5

# The Green We Buried

*They told us to save the forests. We paved them instead.*

You don't even notice it anymore.

That patch of trees you passed on your way to work – it's now a construction site. The park your child used to play in – now a parking lot. That silent stretch of shade between two buildings – now a glass tower under construction.

It didn't happen overnight. It happened while we were busy.

And now, the silence left behind by those trees? It's been replaced by heat. Dust. Noise. And a terrifying truth: We are choking because we buried our green.

## Urban Forests: The Lungs We Cut Out

Forests were never just faraway wilderness. Cities had them too – in parks, along roads, inside campuses, behind colonies. But over time, we gave them up in exchange for "progress."

Let the numbers sink in:

- Delhi lost over 1 million trees between 2001 and 2021 to construction and road widening
- Mumbai lost over 50% of its mangroves since the 1990s
- Bengaluru, once known as "The Garden City," has lost 88% of its green cover since 1973

We didn't just cut trees. We cut air-conditioners gifted by nature, rain magnets, pollution filters, and mental health sanctuaries.

## When a Tree Falls in a City, No One Hears It

Here's what actually happens when a tree is felled:

- Dust levels rise
- Local temperatures increase by 2-4°C
- Rainwater absorption capacity drops
- Birds, insects, and biodiversity disappear
- Residents complain of more cough, fatigue, and irritation

And yet, tree cutting continues across India, often in the name of:

- Flyovers
- Metro rail
- Housing societies
- Government buildings
- "Beautification projects"

The irony?. We're building infrastructure to improve urban life... while destroying what makes urban life livable.

## Forests Are Now Fire Zones

In the past decade, India has seen a sharp spike in forest fires — even in areas that never experienced them before.

In Uttarakhand, forests burn nearly every summer. In Himachal Pradesh, fires now rage for days, destroying both forests and villages. Even parts of Madhya Pradesh and Odisha are reporting climate-induced fires due to rising temperatures and human interference.

India lost over 1,100 sq km of forest cover to fires in 2023 alone.

We're not just letting forests die — we're watching them burn, and doing very little to stop it.

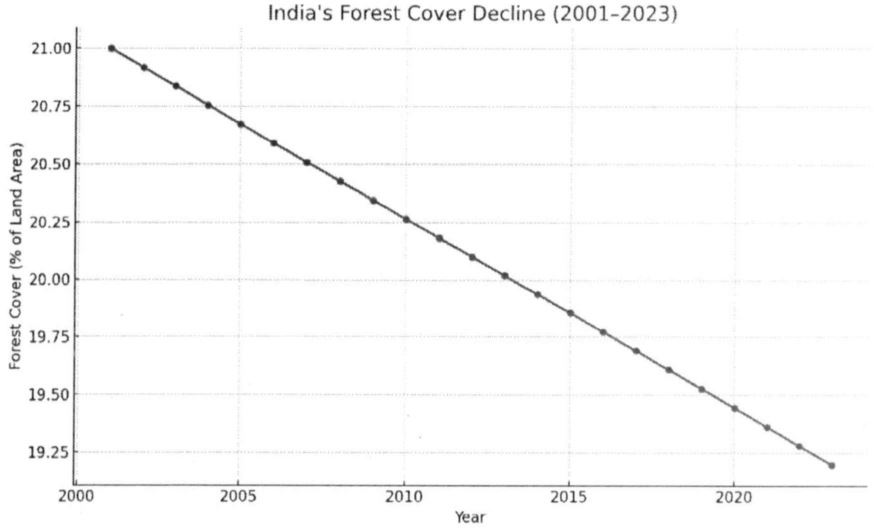


## Trees Regulate Temperature. We Cut That Off.

It's not just about shade. A mature tree can:

- Cool the air around it by up to 5°C
- Absorb 21 kg of $CO_2$ each year
- Hold 100 litres of rainwater in its roots
- Prevent soil erosion and flash flooding

When we remove trees, we don't just lose greenery - we lose climate control mechanisms, we lose natural infrastructure, we lose protection against heat, flood, and pollution.

## Green Cover on Paper ≠ Green Cover on Ground

Government reports often claim "green cover" is increasing. What they don't tell you is:

- This includes commercial plantations (like eucalyptus or palm, which don't support biodiversity)
- Many so-called "green zones" are isolated patches, not real forests
- Satellite data can count even golf courses and lawns as green cover

It's a numbers game - and the real forests are still disappearing.

## Why This Should Terrify Urban Families

Let's talk about what this means for your daily life:

- Your child will grow up without knowing what a real forest feels like
- Your morning walks will become sweaty, smoggy marches through concrete jungles
- Your society park will shrink, or vanish - eaten by parking or a "new block"
- Summer will feel longer, hotter, and more unbearable with each passing year
- Mental health issues like anxiety and stress will spike - because access to green space reduces cortisol levels, and we're removing them.

## The Final Cut

In a 2022 survey, 77% of urban Indians said they "miss the greenery" they grew up with. But nostalgia doesn't plant trees. And guilt doesn't bring them back.

We want ACs, malls, wider roads, faster trains. But where do we want the forests to go?

We bury them under the name of growth. And then complain that we can't breathe.

## What 2035 Could Look Like If We Don't Stop

- Urban zones where temperatures routinely cross 50°C
- Children with no exposure to wildlife beyond screens
- Floods where trees once absorbed the deluge
- City life that feels more like survival - day after day

## A Funeral Without a Body

No sirens go off when a tree is killed. There's no crime scene. No outrage. Just silence.

But the silence is heating up. It's drying the ground. It's choking the air. And in 2035, it might come for your colony, your children, your breath.

## Coming Up Next:

Chapter 6: The Sacred Peaks and Plastic Wrappers

We thought the mountains would remain untouched – silent, sacred, and clean. But even at 13,000 feet, the wrappers crunch beneath our boots.

# Chapter 6

# The Sacred Peaks and Plastic Wrappers

*"We climbed seeking silence, found only packets and Pet bottles."*

**- Parminder Singh**

Parminder Singh has trekked dozens of times. He's not a tourist. He's a pilgrim, an adventurer, and a lover of the mountains. He knows what it's like to breathe thin air, to sleep under stars, and to walk where roads end.

So when he and a group of friends set out for Kailash Manimahesh — one of the most sacred and remote treks in India — they expected spiritual silence, maybe snow, maybe hardship.

They didn't expect **maggie wrappers**, **bisleri bottles**, and **sanitary waste frozen into the glacier**.

They didn't expect to be stepping over **discarded shoes, torn tarps, and gutka pouches** with every few steps.

They didn't expect the Himalayas to feel like a dustbin.

## The Mountains Are Dying Quietly

We often say that India's mountains are spiritual, untouched, timeless. But the truth is, they're choking.

Tourism has exploded — and with it, so has garbage.

- The **Manimahesh Yatra** sees over **4 lakh pilgrims annually**. But there is **no solid waste management system at high altitudes.**

- **Kedarnath, Triund, Roopkund, Valley of Flowers, Spiti,** and **Leh** are drowning in the very thing tourists bring up with them: packaged food, disposable bottles, plastic raincoats, snack wrappers.
- Once left, this waste doesn't decompose. It **freezes.** It **blows into glaciers.** It **leaches into pristine mountain streams.**

What doesn't burn — stays. What doesn't get carried down — rots in the sun. And no one carries it back.

## From Sacred to Sickening

Parminder described one moment in detail.

"We reached this small glacial bend just below the lake. And I kid you not — there were **20-30 empty liquor bottles stacked against a rock**, as if someone held a party there. A party... at 13,000 feet."

Not far from there, they found a torn packet of "diet chips," a broken thermocol sheet, and a sandal.

This wasn't just trash. It was **desecration**.

What was once sacred terrain - now **echoes with the sound of crunching wrappers instead of wind**.

## Data Hidden in Snow

- In 2022, **The Himalayan Cleanup** campaign collected **1.1 lakh kg of waste from 11 mountain states**.
- A 2023 study by the GB Pant Institute found **traces of microplastics in glacial meltwater** across Uttarakhand.
- Over **80% of trash collected during mountain cleanups** is **non-recyclable plastic**, mostly from packaged food.

Tourists bring plastic for convenience. Locals don't have the systems to manage it. The mountain keeps the memory.

### The Myth of "Eco-tourism"

Many trekking companies use terms like "eco" and "sustainable" - but few practice what they preach.

- Porters overloaded with 20 kg of tourist waste.
- Guides burning plastic to reduce carry-back load.
- Campsites dumping leftover packaging into nearby gorges at night.

And worst of all - **pilgrims who think that religious sentiment gives them immunity from responsibility.**

As if faith absolves footprint.

## Why This Should Terrify You in the City

You may think - *so what? It's in the mountains.*

But here's what you're not seeing:

- **80% of North India's water comes from Himalayan glaciers.**
- That plastic in the snow? It will melt into your rivers, your taps, your kitchen.
- **Delhi's Yamuna, Punjab's canals, Haryana's groundwater — all trace back to these frozen sources.**

When you pollute the mountain, **you poison the future** — one slow leak at a time.

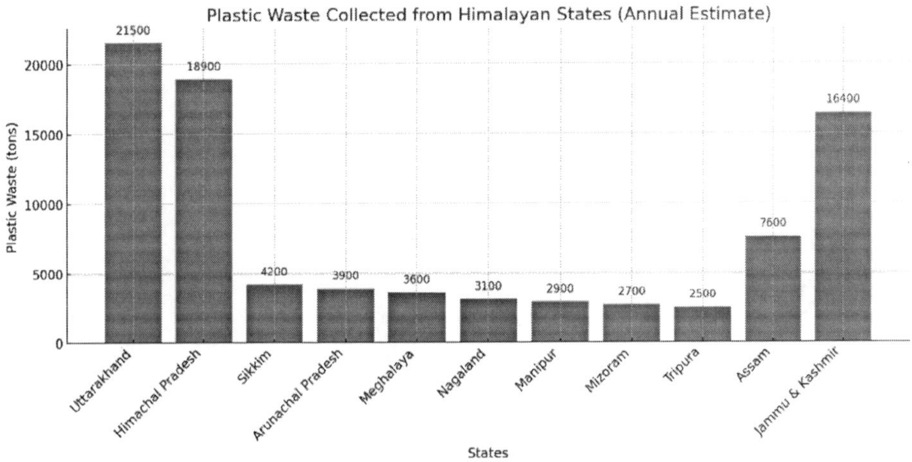


## The Trek That Changed Them

When Parminder and his friends returned, they didn't post pictures.

They held a cleanup drive in their own neighbourhood. They stopped buying packaged trail food. They began carrying trash bags whenever they hiked.

Because the mountain had changed. But more importantly - *they had.*

We romanticise the Himalayas. We write poems, take selfies, chant mantras.

But we've forgotten the most sacred vow: **Leave no trace.**

If our mountains are sacred, then what are we doing to them?

**The next generation won't climb to feel awe.** They'll climb to count bottles. And maybe, one day, to bury what's left.

## Coming Up Next:

Chapter 7: Plastic Nation

How the land beneath our feet and the blood in our veins are slowly filling with microplastics — and why escaping it may no longer be an option.

# Chapter 7

# Plastic Nation

*It's in your food. It's in your water. It's in your blood.*

You finish your meal and throw away the container. You feel good - it's going to recycling, right?

Wrong.

That plastic box you just tossed will likely:

- Be dumped in a landfill
- Burnt in an open fire
- Or worse - broken down into tiny pieces that will enter someone's lungs, blood, or brain

You see, plastic doesn't disappear. It mutates - into invisible poisons. And today, India isn't just surrounded by plastic. We've become it.

## The Plastic Flood: No City Spared

India generates over 3.5 million tonnes of plastic waste every year - and over 40% of it is single-use.

Think about it:

- Food wrappers
- E-commerce packaging
- Shampoo sachets
- Grocery bags

- Bottled water
- Disposable cutlery
- Medical syringes, straws, and spoons

It's everywhere. In cities. In rivers. In the stomachs of cows, dogs, birds. And now, in you.

## Microplastics: The New Toxin You Can't Avoid

Microplastics are plastic fragments smaller than 5mm. They're so tiny, they've entered:

- Drinking water
- Sea salt and sugar
- Human blood and breast milk
- Fruits and vegetables (through polluted soil and irrigation water)

A study by the International Pollutants Elimination Network (IPEN) in 2023 found microplastics in 100% of blood samples collected from Indian adults in urban cities.

Yes - every person tested had plastic in their bloodstream.

And no, scientists still don't fully understand the long-term effects. But initial findings link microplastics to:

- Hormonal imbalance
- Liver and kidney dysfunction
- Fertility issues
- Increased cancer risk
- Neurological damage

We are literally becoming plastic people.

## Burn It, Bury It, or Dump It — You Still Lose

Here's the nightmare:

- If you burn plastic, it releases dioxins - deadly toxins that can cause cancer and genetic damage
- If you dump plastic, it clogs drains and rivers - leading to floods and water contamination
- If you recycle plastic, it still eventually ends up in the environment - because most Indian cities don't have advanced facilities

Even "recyclable" plastic is often not truly recycled - especially multi-layered packaging used by chips, biscuits, and cosmetics brands.

These go straight to incinerators, where they poison the air in low-income neighborhoods.

The rich generate plastic. The poor inhale it.

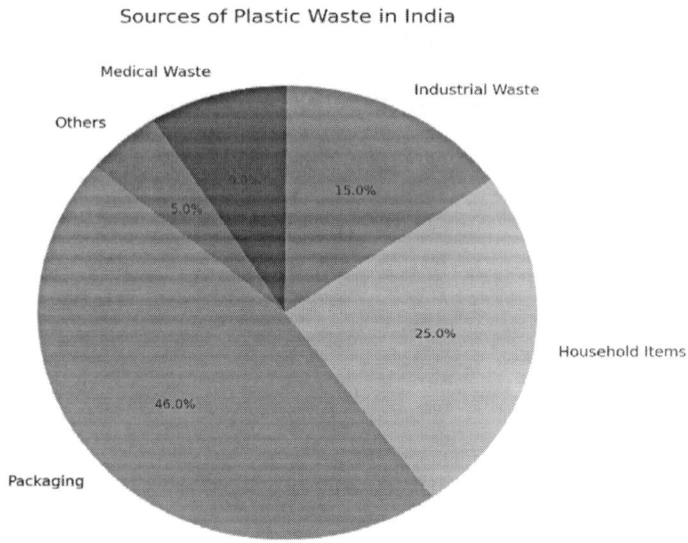

## Urban India: A Plastic Jungle

In Delhi-NCR, Yamuna is now called a plastic river. In Mumbai, Versova beach had over 12,000 tonnes of plastic removed in just one clean-up. In Bengaluru, Bellandur Lake literally caught fire because of industrial waste mixed with floating plastic.

Your city may look clean. But scratch the surface — and the plastic is piling up just below your feet.

## Children and Plastic Exposure: A Toxic Bond

- Toys made of cheap, unregulated plastic leach BPA and phthalates
- Milk bottles, lunch boxes, and even water bottles marketed as "kid-friendly" often contain hormone disruptors
- Children's bodies absorb more toxins per kilogram than adults - making plastic exposure far more dangerous for them

By the time your child turns 10, they've already ingested thousands of plastic particles - through food, water, or air.

## The E-commerce Boom = A Plastic Apocalypse

Every online order comes with a cost: Bubble wrap. Air pillows. Polybags. Tape. Disposable pouches.

India's e-commerce sector shipped more than 8 billion packages in 2023, with plastic packaging accounting for over 60% of the material used.

And here's the twist: 99% of this plastic is non-recyclable.

Convenience today. Contamination forever.

## Plastic-Free? That's a Lie.

Even if you live consciously - say no to straws, use cloth bags, carry your bottle - you're still not plastic-free.

Why?

Because:

- Your vegetables were stored in crates lined with plastic sheets
- Your milk came in plastic pouches
- Your RO filter uses a plastic membrane
- Your toothpaste tube is unrecyclable

It's not about individual guilt..It's about a system that's designed to wrap everything in plastic — and leave you with no way out.

## 2035: What a Plastic Nation Looks Like

- Toxic air due to more plastic incineration
- Contaminated crops because plastic particles are now in the soil
- Seafood bans as oceans choke with polymer waste
- Plastic-related illnesses becoming common - infertility, organ damage, behavioral disorders
- The rise of "plastic poverty" - where the poor suffer the most because their surroundings become dumping grounds

## Not Surrounding Us - Consuming Us

We used to worry about plastic around us. The real fear now? It's inside us.

In our blood. Our lungs. Our unborn children. And no filter, no lifestyle upgrade, no app can fully protect us.

We didn't just bury the green. We replaced it with toxic, permanent plastic.

And unless we stop it, Bharat 2035 won't just be a plastic nation - It'll be a plastic generation.

## Coming Up Next:

Chapter 8 : The Price of Convenience

From food delivery apps to fast fashion and disposable everything — our comfort comes at a deadly cost.

It's a silent trade-off where the planet pays the price for our ease.

# Chapter 8

## The Price of Convenience

*Every shortcut we took is now turning against us*

What made life easier is now making the planet unlivable.

We wanted comfort. We got collapse.

Somewhere between our need for speed and our love for ease, we signed an invisible contract: "Make my life simpler - no matter the cost."

Now, the cost has arrived.

Not on our bank statements. But in the air we breathe. The water we drink. The food we eat. The silence of the birds. The heat in our homes.

And we still don't realise... our lifestyle *is* the crisis.

Wake up. Brew a Nespresso pod. Tap a button - breakfast delivered. Drive in your air-conditioned car. Eat lunch wrapped in cling film. Return home, order groceries online. Switch on the AC. Plug in the devices. Stream a show.

Sounds harmless, right?

Now zoom out.

- Each delivery = vehicle emissions + plastic packaging + warehousing waste
- Each pod = single-use plastic + energy-intensive aluminum
- Each online order = overproduction + returns waste + fuel

- Each cool blast = rising electricity demand + urban heat dumping

We've turned basic actions into climate weapons. Not out of malice. But convenience.

## The Comfort Industry

Convenience is now a trillion-dollar industry:

- Zomato and Swiggy make over 4 million deliveries per day
- Quick-commerce apps like Blinkit and Zepto promise groceries in 10 minutes
- India's e-commerce is projected to cross $200 billion by 2027, with plastic packaging waste doubling every 3-4 years

None of this comes with eco-limits.

- Delivery bikes idle in traffic - burning fuel
- Groceries are triple-packaged even a lemon comes in plastic
- Returns are often burned or landfilled, not reused

We've built a system where "fast" means fossil fuels, and "easy" means emissions.

## The Cold That's Heating Us Up

Air-conditioners are now everywhere - homes, cabs, shops, hospitals, classrooms.

By 2030, India is expected to have over 1 billion cooling devices, leading to:

- A 4x spike in electricity demand
- Rising greenhouse gases like HFCs (which are thousands of times more potent than $CO_2$)

- Urban heat dumping - where outdoor temperatures rise as millions of ACs blast heat into the streets

So the hotter it gets, the more ACs we use. And the more ACs we use, the hotter it gets.

This is not cooling. It's climate suicide.

## Bottled Water. Packaged Air

We don't trust what's free anymore. We want purity - but only if it's in plastic.

- India consumes over 14 billion litres of bottled water annually
- Most of it comes in non-recyclable bottles
- 90% of plastic bottles are not recycled - they're dumped, burnt, or buried

We've made water a luxury. And plastic - a necessity.

Some startups are now selling canned "pure mountain air" in Delhi and Gurgaon. What was once free and abundant… now comes with an MRP.

That's not innovation. That's desperation in a can.

## One Meal, Three Problems

Ordering a ₹250 thali? You're also getting:

1. Plastic packaging (not recyclable)
2. Delivery emissions from a petrol bike
3. Food waste (most outlets discard leftovers every night)

Multiply that by 5 crore food orders a day - and you have a full-blown sustainability disaster.

The saddest part? Most people order food not out of hunger - but boredom.

We're trading the future of our planet... for convenience we barely needed.

## The Real Cost Isn't on the Receipt

Convenience comes cheap - but only to us.

The real price is paid by:

- Children with lung damage
- Rivers choking with plastic
- Animals dying of starvation with stomachs full of wrappers
- Farmers walking miles because their borewell is dry
- Delivery riders collapsing during heatwaves to fulfill our 10-minute needs

We aren't bad people. We're just trained to not look

## But Why Do We Still Choose This?

Because the system was built to keep us blind.

- You don't see the landfill where your packaging ends up
- You don't meet the delivery guy gasping in 46°C heat
- You don't hear the bee that doesn't come back

Convenience hides the consequence.

Until it doesn't.

Until the water stops.

Until the air stings.

Until the food tastes funny.

Until the silence outside is no longer peaceful — it's permanent.

## The Irony?

Most of what we call "convenience" today... ...was not a problem 20 years ago.

- We carried steel tiffins
- Bought groceries with cloth bags
- Ate home-cooked food
- Lived without 24x7 AC
- Walked to buy milk

We didn't call it "sustainable." It was just normal.

Now we call this normal a trend. Eco-friendly. Conscious. Ethical.

We rebrand survival... while dying slowly.

## Final Warning: Your Comfort Is Killing You

If Bharat 2035 collapses, it won't be because of oil barons or bad policies alone. It'll be because millions of people chose plastic forks over reusable ones.

It'll be because we mistook comfort for progress.

And by the time we understand the real price of convenience...

It might be too late to pay it back.

## Coming Up Next:

Chapter 9: Soil to Sickness

How poisoned soil, pesticide overload, and dying biodiversity are silently killing what's on your plate - and inside your body.

# Chapter 9

# Soil to Sickness

*The journey from dying earth to dying bodies.*

Your plate looks perfect. Golden rotis. Fresh vegetables. Fragrant rice. Crunchy salad.

But what if you knew:

- That wheat was grown on land laced with arsenic
- That the vegetables were sprayed with chlorpyrifos, a neurotoxin banned in many countries
- That the rice came from fields irrigated by sewage water mixed with industrial waste

Would it still taste the same?

Because in Bharat 2035, the real danger is no longer in the air or the water. It's in the soil beneath our food - and the sickness silently entering through every bite.

## The Land Is Dying. Quietly.

India's farmland is not as fertile as it once was.

Over 30% of Indian soil is now degraded - eroded, nutrient-depleted, or poisoned. The reasons?

- Overuse of chemical fertilizers and pesticides
- Excessive mono-cropping (same crop, same season, year after year)

- Shrinking organic content - compost and natural waste replaced by synthetic sprays
- Unscientific irrigation practices that flood land with salts and heavy metals

Soil, which once teemed with earthworms, microbes, and life - is now often a sterile powder, barely holding on.

And yet... it still grows our food.

## From Fertile to Fatal

We've turned our soil into a toxic sponge.

Here's what's getting absorbed:

- Urea, DAP, and synthetic nitrogen fertilizers - overused to boost quick yields
- Pesticides banned in developed countries - but still legal and heavily used in India
- Heavy metals from industrial discharge - like lead, cadmium, and arsenic
- Untreated sewage used for irrigation in peri-urban farms

These don't stay in the soil.

They're absorbed by:

- Vegetables like spinach, cauliflower, and brinjal
- Grains like wheat and rice
- Fruits sprayed with ripening chemicals like calcium carbide

And from there - into your bloodstream.

## We're Eating the Problem

A few horrifying facts:

- Over 50% of fruits and vegetables in urban Indian markets show pesticide residue
- A study by AIIMS (2022) detected high levels of lead and mercury in spinach sold across Delhi
- In Punjab's "cancer belt," 1 in 3 households have someone battling pesticide-related illness
- The pesticide chlorpyrifos - linked to brain damage in children - is still widely used in Indian farms

This isn't rural news. This is your city, your sabzi mandi, your child's lunchbox.

## Farmers at the Frontline of Poison

The people growing your food? They're suffering first.

- Over 20,000 pesticide poisoning cases are reported annually in India — many leading to death
- Farmers in Maharashtra, Punjab, and Andhra Pradesh regularly spray without masks or gloves
- Some states still promote endosulfan — a chemical banned globally, linked to birth defects

And in desperation to save crops, more chemicals are sprayed than ever before — even as the soil screams in silence.

## Organic? Often Just a Label

Urban Indians are switching to "organic" food. But most don't know:

- There is no strict enforcement of organic certification in India
- "100% organic" products can still legally contain up to 5% pesticide residue
- Many brands source from the same wholesalers who supply to conventional markets

So yes, you might be paying triple - But still eating toxins. Just beautifully packaged.

## The Youngest Are Most Vulnerable

- Children absorb pesticides faster and retain them longer
- Early exposure can lead to developmental delays, autoimmune disorders, and cancer risks
- Even breast milk samples in polluted areas have shown chemical residue
- School lunch programs and tiffins often use vegetables soaked in chemical pesticides from bulk mandis

Your child isn't safe from this crisis. They may be the first generation to grow up fully surrounded by edible poisons.

## Biodiversity Breakdown

Pesticides and soil degradation are also killing:

- Bees and pollinators - essential for over 70% of our food crops
- Earthworms and beneficial insects - nature's natural fertilisers

- Native crop varieties - replaced by high-yield, chemically dependent hybrids

What we lose isn't just nutrition - We lose resilience, diversity, and taste.

The bajra your grandmother ate doesn't exist anymore. The tomato you eat today is a flavourless, chemical-soaked clone.

## 2035: What's Coming to Your Plate

- Pesticide-resistant super pests
- Rising food allergies, especially in children
- Sharp spikes in early-age cancers linked to contaminated produce
- Chronic diseases (thyroid, infertility, neurological disorders) becoming common in 30s and 40s
- Food grown in hydroponic labs for the rich - while the poor eat what the soil has become

## Not Just Hunger - But Harm

India fought a long battle to eliminate hunger. But in 2035, the new crisis is this:

We may have enough food - ...but that food may be killing us slowly.

From soil to harvest. From harvest to kitchen. From your kitchen to your bloodstream. The sickness is silent. But it's spreading.

And no one told you the soil was the starting point.

## Coming Up Next:

Chapter 10: The Air We Inhale, The Lives We Exhale

It's not just pollution - it's slow asphyxiation. How invisible poisons in urban air are now linked to heart attacks, infertility, and dementia.

# Chapter 10

# The Air We Inhale, The Lives We Exhale

*It doesn't smell. It doesn't burn. But it's killing you anyway.*

You step outside and take a breath. Seems normal.

But inside that breath are:

- PM2.5 particles smaller than a blood cell
- Nitrogen dioxide from vehicles
- Volatile organic compounds (VOCs) from paints and perfumes
- Formaldehyde, benzene, ozone, and in some cities – arsenic and lead

Still seems normal?

Every day, with every breath, we are inhaling disease. Not because we smoke. But because we live in urban India.

## India's Urban Air: A Daily Dose of Death

- 38 out of the world's 50 most polluted cities are in India
- In Delhi, air quality levels during winter cross 500 AQI - more than 10x the safe limit
- Cities like Kanpur, Patna, Lucknow, Gurugram, and Ghaziabad consistently rank among the worst
- Even smaller towns like Firozabad, Varanasi, and Agra now report hazardous air year-round

It's not just a smoggy skyline. It's a toxic dome that we walk, sleep, eat, work, and raise children under.

## What's In The Air - and What It's Doing to You

*Key pollutants:*

- PM2.5 & PM10: Particulate matter that enters lungs, blood, even the brain
- $NO_2$ & $SO_2$: Gases from vehicles and power plants - triggers for asthma, heart disease
- $O_3$ (Ozone): Not the protective kind - this one damages lung tissue
- Carbon monoxide: Reduces oxygen in the bloodstream, especially dangerous indoors

*The result:*

- Rising cases of stroke, heart attacks, and lung cancer
- Surge in respiratory illnesses in children - bronchitis, asthma, chronic cough
- Infertility, low sperm counts, and miscarriages now linked to long-term exposure
- Early signs of cognitive decline - memory loss, depression, anxiety
- Doctors now say breathing Delhi air is like smoking 10–15 cigarettes a day

## The First Breath Could Be The Most Damaging

Children are the first to suffer:

- They breathe faster than adults
- Their lungs are still developing
- Their immune systems are weaker
- They live closer to the ground - where the air is often more toxic

In 2022, the Lancet Planetary Health report estimated that over 160,000 children under 5 died in India due to air pollution.

This isn't hypothetical. This is genocide by neglect.

## Your Car Is The Killer You Didn't See Coming

Urban families often believe they're safe inside their cars.

The truth?

- Air inside cars, especially in traffic, can be up to 10x more polluted
- Idling engines release carbon monoxide and diesel particulates right at nose level
- Even luxury vehicles recycle the same toxic air inside a closed cabin

Every school bus, every Ola/Uber, every delivery bike - adds to a growing cloud of death.

And we contribute to it every day, often without realizing it.

## Indoor Air: The Silent Murderer

You think your home is safe?

Indoor pollution is now a major killer - especially in urban apartments with low ventilation:

- Cooking gas emissions, especially in poorly ventilated kitchens
- Mosquito coils, incense sticks, air fresheners - loaded with VOCs
- Paints, furniture polish, and cleaning sprays - release carcinogens
- Even new furniture can off-gas formaldehyde for months

The World Health Organization estimates that indoor air kills more than 120,000 Indians each year.

You escape traffic to come home. But death might be waiting inside.

## No Organ Is Safe

- Heart: Chronic exposure increases risk of heart attacks and strokes by up to 25–30%
- Lungs: Even healthy non-smokers are developing COPD (Chronic Obstructive Pulmonary Disease)
- Brain: Links to Alzheimer's and dementia now confirmed in long-term exposure zones
- Skin: Pollutants damage the skin barrier, speeding up aging, acne, and dermatitis
- Reproductive system: Sperm quality, menstrual health, and fertility rates are falling in polluted metros

We thought pollution causes cough. But it's also quietly causing organ failure.

## Real People. Real Consequences.

Anita, 29, lives in Delhi and works remotely. She has never smoked. But now suffers from chronic breathlessness and insomnia. Her doctor said: "Just move out. Or buy an oxygen concentrator."

Rishi, 6, studies in a Noida school near an expressway. He uses an inhaler thrice a day. He's never known life without one.

Satish, 42, an Uber driver in Gurugram, developed persistent coughing, fatigue, and chest tightness. He can't afford treatment. He keeps driving - and inhaling.

My wife, Radhika, lived through this nightmare - night after night. For nearly two years, she coughed through every single night, often waking up gasping for breath. There were no fireworks, no viruses, no infections - just air. Air so toxic it felt like poison. It wasn't a bad phase. It was a brutal reality that pushed us to consider something unthinkable: leaving Delhi. The very city we were born in, the city where our work, memories, and loved ones lived — felt like it was trying to evict us one breath at a time. She couldn't step out for work. We stopped going out with friends. Festivals turned into sealed-door weekends with air purifiers working overtime.

One trip to **Ranthambore**, meant to be a relaxing getaway, turned into a full-blown emergency. Her allergy was triggered so severely by the surrounding air and dust that she coughed uncontrollably through the night. Around 2 a.m., I rushed through the sleepy town looking for a medical store - only to find everything shut. Desperation is roaming unfamiliar streets with a phone flashlight, praying a shutter might open. Luckily, I found one that was open — and somehow got my hands on a **nebulizer**. She sat there, in a hotel room far from home, with a plastic mask strapped to her face, breathing through steam and panic. That trip was supposed to be two nights. We returned after one. Because the air was not just suffocating her — it was breaking both of us.

Thankfully, after two painful years, she recovered with medical help. But the scars linger — and so does the air that caused them.

## The Cost of Breathing

In 2023, India lost over $36 billion in economic productivity due to air pollution-related illnesses.

And the long-term cost?

- More hospitalizations
- Lower life expectancy (Delhi residents are losing 9.7 years on average)
- Mental health deterioration
- Chronic dependency on medication and oxygen therapy

Soon, air purifiers won't be a luxury. They'll be a necessity - like clean water once was.

## 2035: A Nation Gasping

- Schools with indoor air shelters
- Office buildings with oxygen chambers for breaks
- Rise in "air migrants" - people moving from cities to hills, not for views, but for survival
- Asthma and bronchitis clinics in every residential block

- Face masks becoming permanent lifestyle accessories

We imagined the future as clean, high-tech, and bright. But right now, 2035 looks gray, wheezing, and covered in smog.

## You Can't Opt Out of Air

You can choose organic food. You can avoid plastic. But you can't stop breathing.

And if the very air you need to live is what's killing you - then what does survival even look like?

## Coming Up Next:

Chapter 11: The Unliveable City

India is turning into a furnace. This chapter explores how rising urban heat is destroying cities, lives, and mental health - one unbearable summer at a time.

# Chapter 11

# The Unliveable City

*When your address becomes your enemy.*

There's no breeze. No shade. No relief. You wake up sweating. You sleep sweating. You walk outside and the heat hits you like a wall. It's not just uncomfortable - it's hostile.

This isn't weather anymore. This is climate violence. And it's sweeping across urban India faster than we can comprehend.

## India Is Heating Up - And It's Not Subtle Anymore

- India experienced its hottest February in over 100 years in 2023
- In 2024, over 37 cities recorded temperatures above 45°C
- Rajasthan hit 50°C multiple times - a mark once considered extreme, now disturbingly routine
- Delhi's Najafgarh recorded 52.9°C in June 2024 - the highest ever in Indian history (now under review)

These aren't just numbers. These are death sentences for the vulnerable, and slow torture for the rest.

## It Doesn't Affect Everyone Equally

In every Indian city:

- The rich crank up their ACs
- The poor sleep on rooftops, tin sheds, or crowded rooms
- Delivery boys, guards, street vendors - they don't get to hide from the sun
- Hospitals fill up with cases of heat exhaustion, dehydration, and stroke

The inequality of heat is brutal. Your PIN code decides your suffering.

## Heatwaves Are the New Silent Killer

According to India's National Disaster Management Authority:

- Between 1992 and 2022, over 25,000 people died due to heatwaves
- But the actual number may be far higher - many deaths go unreported or misattributed to cardiac arrest or "natural causes"
- 2024 saw over 120 deaths in Bihar and Odisha alone within two weeks of extreme heat

And the worst part? Most of these deaths are preventable. We just didn't care enough.

## Your City Is a Giant Oven

Urban areas are now heat islands - meaning they are several degrees hotter than surrounding rural zones. Why?

- Concrete buildings and roads trap heat all day and release it at night
- Loss of tree cover reduces natural cooling
- ACs dump hot air outside, making cities even warmer
- Vehicle and industry emissions create a heat blanket that traps radiation

This means your city is not just warming with the planet - It's amplifying it.

## Heat Doesn't Just Kill the Body. It Destroys the Mind

High temperatures are now linked to:

- Mood swings, irritability, aggression
- Sleep disruption and exhaustion
- Reduced cognitive performance
- Increased risk of suicide and depression
- Poor memory and learning in schoolchildren

A Harvard study found that students performed significantly worse in exams during heatwaves - even when classrooms had fans.

Brains don't function well in boiling rooms. But that's exactly what our schools, offices, and homes are becoming.

## Real People, Real Heat Trauma

Pintu, 17, a food delivery boy in Delhi, fainted mid-shift. The temperature was 47°C. He'd already done 8 deliveries in the heat. His employer marked him "inactive."

Maya, 62, a homemaker in Nagpur, suffered a heatstroke while cooking lunch. The kitchen didn't have a fan – the LPG heat added to the 48°C ambient temperature. She survived. Barely.

Rafiq, 35, a construction worker in Ahmedabad, works with hot cement from 9 am to 5 pm. No shade. No hydration. He now has chronic migraines and heat-triggered seizures.

Heat isn't abstract. It's happening. It's hitting. It's hurting.

## We're Not Designed for This

The human body begins to fail at:

- Over 40°C body temperature
- Prolonged dehydration
- Continuous exposure to hot surfaces and air

India's workers, delivery agents, traffic cops, and daily wage labourers routinely face these extremes - with no legal protection, no heat safety codes, and no sick leave.

If this were a war, they'd be the frontliners. But this is climate collapse - and they're dying in silence.

## And It's Only Getting Worse

IPCC projections say that by 2035:

- India will experience up to 150 extremely hot days per year
- Large cities may see daytime highs of 55°C by mid-century
- Urban power demand for cooling will triple - but infrastructure will lag
- Water scarcity will exponentially rise during summer due to evaporation and overuse

This means:

- More blackouts
- Higher electricity bills
- Water cuts during peak heat
- And a permanent sense of unlivable summer fatigue

## There's No Escape Anymore

You can't "just stay indoors." You can't "drink more water and rest."

Because:

- Your walls trap heat
- Your fan blows hot air
- Your city no longer cools at night

Heat has crept into your home, your sleep, your blood pressure. And soon, your child may grow up thinking 50°C is just summer.

This is not an extreme. It's becoming the baseline.

## Coming Up Next:

Chapter 12: Water Wars

From housing societies to rivers, from tankers to taps - this chapter dives into the brutal fights, theft, and politics of water in India's hottest decade yet.

# Chapter 12

# Water Wars

*The next fight isn't for land. It's for your next glass of water.*

There's a knock on your door at 5 a.m.

It's your neighbor.

"We didn't get any water today. Can we borrow a few buckets?"

You say yes. But silently wonder — what if you run out too?

This isn't a scene from a drought-ridden village. It's urban India in 2035 — where water isn't just scarce... It's a currency, a conflict, a crisis.

## Taps That Run Dry, Every Day

In cities like Delhi, Chennai, Bengaluru, and Hyderabad:

- Water availability has dropped to less than 100 litres per person per day - below WHO minimums
- 50-70% of households now rely on private tankers
- Illegal borewells are tapping into dead aquifers
- Many colonies receive water for just 30 minutes a day - sometimes less

And in slums or lower-income areas, it's worse.

No schedule. No pressure. No explanation.

Just silence - and empty buckets.

## The Tanker Mafia Is In Control

Water is a basic right. But in many Indian cities, it's a black market business.

- In parts of Delhi, tanker operators charge ₹2,000–₹4,000 for 5,000 litres
- In Bengaluru, apartment complexes have signed monthly contracts with tanker lobbies
- In Chennai, gangs bribe officials to divert municipal supply
- In Pune, housing societies bid against each other for early delivery slots

It's not about who needs water. It's about who can pay more for it.

## Groundwater: The Vanishing Lifeline

India is the world's largest extractor of groundwater, using over 25% of global reserves.

But now:

- 21 major Indian cities will run out of groundwater by 2030 (NITI Aayog)
- In Delhi, groundwater levels have dropped by 10 meters in just a decade
- Borewells are being dug up to 300-400 feet deep, bringing up fluoride, arsenic, and heavy metals

It's not just water scarcity. It's water poisoning.

The more we dig, the more we rot.

## The Housing Society Crisis

What was once a luxury - gated societies with 24/7 water - is now a battleground.

- Tankers arrive late, or not at all
- Residents fight over who gets to fill buckets first
- Borewell systems collapse in summer months
- Builders promise "water security" - and deliver broken pipes and unpaid bills

Even in posh apartments, people are storing water in plastic drums, skipping showers, and installing sensors to ration flushing.

Because comfort means nothing without water.

## Water Quality? That's Another Crisis.

If you're lucky enough to get water, there's no guarantee it's safe.

- Over 70% of India's surface water is now contaminated
- Tap water in many cities contains E. coli, nitrates, and industrial effluents
- RO filters are everywhere - but they waste 3-4 litres for every litre purified
- In some places, water supplied by tankers is simply treated sewage - not safe for drinking

Clean water is no longer a birthright. It's a luxury service.

## The Economic Cost of a Water-Starved City

Water scarcity doesn't just hit homes. It cripples economies.

- Industries like textiles, beverages, and IT cooling systems are seeing massive operational losses
- Hospitals have faced water shutdowns during summer peaks
- Schools and offices are reducing working hours
- Daily wage workers, car washers, vegetable vendors - all lose income when water runs out

No water = No productivity.

## Real People. Real Loss.

Amrita, 33, lost her father in Delhi to heatstroke and dehydration. The colony didn't get water for two days. The tankers were redirected to a VIP area.

Asha, 14, in a Mumbai slum, walks 2.5 km each morning just to fill two buckets before school. She's missed over 30 school days this year - not due to illness, but due to water collection.

## 2035: What Water Wars Will Look Like

- Housing societies hiring private security to guard tanker water
- Apps that let you book underground water like cab rides
- Neighborhoods physically fighting over pipeline cuts and diversions
- Crime and corruption around water theft
- Children falling ill from untreated tanker water

And eventually:

- Migration from cities not because of jobs - but because of thirst

## Water Is Power. And Power Is Now Scarce.

Forget gold. Forget land.

The real war of the future is being fought for something you once let run while brushing your teeth.

And the scariest part?

We still haven't understood the scale of what's coming.

## Coming Up Next:

Chapter 13: The Last Roar

A haunting look at how the collapse of India's wildlife and biodiversity is not just an environmental loss - but a direct threat to food, climate, and urban life.

# Chapter 13

# The Last Roar

*When forests fall silent, cities start to scream.*

It was just one tiger.

One leopard.

One forest patch.

One dry stream.

One silent jungle.

But now - multiply that silence by millions. And it becomes a scream.

Because in 2035, the wild isn't just dying in forests. It's collapsing in your life, your air, your food, and your future.

## India: Once a Biodiversity Giant, Now Shrinking Fast

India is home to:

- Over 500 species of mammals
- 1,300+ birds, 300+ reptiles, and 400+ amphibians
- 4 major global biodiversity hotspots

But this richness is disappearing at record speed:

- 10% of India's wildlife species are already endangered
- Tiger corridors are shrinking, and their prey is vanishing
- Wetlands are drying. Rivers are choking. Birds are missing.

- Over 200 species of birds, butterflies, and frogs have vanished from urban India in the last 2 decades

This is not normal. This is not "development." This is ecological collapse in slow motion.

## The Tiger Is Still Here - But Barely

India often boasts of having the largest wild tiger population in the world.

But let's be honest:

- Over 93% of original tiger habitat is gone
- Tigers are now trapped in fragmented forest islands, unable to roam or breed freely
- Roadways, mines, and cities have cut through key tiger corridors
- And human-tiger conflict is rising - because we left them no choice

The last roar may not come from the jungle. It may come from a cage. Or worse - a museum.

## Where Did the Birds Go?

Open your window.

Remember the sparrows? Gone.

The cuckoo in summer?

Silent.

The bulbul, koel, mynah, hornbill? Rare sightings now — if you're lucky.

Why?

- Loss of native trees
- Towers and glass buildings disrupting flight paths
- Pesticide-laced crops killing insects (their food)
- Noise pollution confusing their calls and mating cycles

Birds were never just for beauty. They pollinated, they signaled seasons, they controlled pests.

And now, we're paying the price for their silence.

## The Buzz Is Gone - and So Is the Food

Bees, butterflies, and insects are disappearing too.

Globally, pollinator populations have dropped by 40–60%. In India, entire bee colonies are collapsing due to:

- Pesticide exposure
- Climate change
- Habitat destruction
- Monoculture farming

No bees = no pollination.

No pollination = no fruits, no vegetables, no seeds.

You may have money for food. But soon, there may be no food to buy.

## Elephants, Leopards, and Monkeys in Your Backyard?

In 2023–24 alone:

- Over 900 human-wildlife conflict incidents were reported across India
- Elephants entered highways, farms, railway tracks - and were often killed
- Leopards walked into gated colonies in Gurugram, Mumbai, Dehradun
- Monkeys in Himachal, Rajasthan, and Delhi have become aggressive urban gangs

Why is this happening?

Because we've taken their land. Destroyed their food sources. And left them with nowhere to go - but into our chaos.

## The Vanishing Forests

Between 2001 and 2023:

- India lost over 2.3 million hectares of tree cover (Global Forest Watch)
- This equals an area larger than Mizoram and Sikkim combined
- Dense forests were replaced by commercial plantations, highways, and "smart cities"
- Even "green cover" in reports is often non-native species or golf courses

Forests aren't just trees. They're lungs, sponges, filters, and sanctuaries.

Remove them - and everything collapses:

- Air pollution rises
- Carbon storage drops
- Temperature spikes
- Diseases jump from animals to humans

Yes, even pandemics are linked to forest destruction. Ask any virologist.

## Biodiversity Loss = Death By A Thousand Cuts

You don't feel it immediately. That's the danger.

But slowly, biodiversity loss begins to:

- Ruin food chains
- Make cities hotter
- Kill off pest controllers
- Destroy the soil's natural balance
- Invite floods, droughts, landslides
- Make viruses jump species more easily

Nature is not decorative. It's defensive.

And when you erase it - there's no Plan B.

## It's Not Just About Wildlife. It's About You.

You may never see a pangolin.

Or a Himalayan vulture.

Or a Nilgiri langur.

But their loss still affects:

- The air you breathe
- The food you eat
- The floods that ruin your home
- The diseases that find their way into your lungs

When the wild disappears, nature doesn't vanish. It retaliates.

## The Jungle Is Bleeding. So Are We.

The last roar of the tiger may not be heard.

But in the silence that follows, we'll hear something else:

- Children falling ill more often
- Crops failing with no pollinators
- Cities drowning or burning
- And a planet that's too unbalanced to support us anymore

We always thought nature was "out there." In forests. In reserves. On TV.

But the truth is harsh: What vanishes from the jungle comes back as pain in the city.

## Coming Up Next:

Chapter 14: The Edge of Collapse

A powerful wrap-up chapter — pulling together everything we've ignored, feared, and denied — and showing how close Bharat 2035 is to irreversible tipping points.

# Chapter 14

# The Edge of Collapse

*Not tomorrow. Not someday. The fall is already in motion.*

There's no one explosion. No one blackout. No one flood.

Collapse doesn't arrive like a movie climax. It slips in - one cracked pipe, one heatwave, one breathless child at a time.

And by the time you realise the system is breaking - you're already inside the fall.

This is not the future. This is *Bharat 2035.*

And we are standing one step away from the irreversible.

## Everything Is Connected. And Breaking Together.

Let's join the dots:

- The heat makes water evaporate faster
- Water shortages force more people to rely on tankers and groundwater
- Overdrawn groundwater weakens soil, ruins crops, and invites land subsidence
- Contaminated crops make people sick, while polluted air makes recovery impossible
- Loss of forests and biodiversity accelerates flooding, diseases, and food chain collapse

- Meanwhile, urban expansion pushes wildlife into cities, and poor waste management spreads new illnesses

It's not one crisis. It's a chain reaction.

And each link is rusting.

## Cities on the Brink

Cities were built for growth. But now, they're cracking under their own weight.

- Delhi: Choking air, dying rivers, water theft, waste mountains
- Bengaluru: Lakes catching fire, groundwater exhausted, traffic emissions rising
- Mumbai: Annual flooding, rising sea levels, vanishing mangroves
- Chennai: Day Zero water threats, heat spikes, saline groundwater
- Gurgaon, Noida, Pune: Dust bowls with glass towers - built too fast, planned too little

And it's spreading to Tier 2 and Tier 3 cities - fast.

India is not just urbanising. It's urbanising into disaster.

## Tipping Points: No U-Turns Beyond These

Here's what scientists mean by "tipping points" - moments after which the damage cannot be reversed, no matter what we do.

India is already close to several:

- Air Quality Tipping Point: When lungs start failing across generations

- Heat Tolerance Threshold: Beyond which outdoor work becomes fatal
- Water Table Collapse: Aquifers that take hundreds of years to recharge being emptied in decades
- Soil Sterility: Land that can't grow crops, even with fertilizers
- Species Extinction Cascade: One species gone triggers many more to follow

These aren't theoretical. These are active countdowns - some with only 5–10 years left.

## This Isn't Just Environmental. It's Personal.

This collapse is not in the Himalayas. It's not in the Amazon.

It's:

- In your child's asthma inhaler
- In the ₹4,000 monthly RO water bill
- In the extra fan you bought last summer
- In the dirty vegetables on your dinner table
- In the quiet resignation of your ageing parents who say, *"humare time mein aisa nahi hota tha"*

This is not *out there*. This is *in here*. With us. Now.

## The Economy Will Bleed Next

Environmental collapse comes with a bill:

- Medical costs skyrocketing
- Productivity falling due to heat and disease
- Tourism crashing due to unsafe air and water

- Insurance rates rising for homes in flood or heat-risk zones
- Food inflation from crop failures and pesticide bans

By 2035, India risks losing up to 3% of its GDP annually due to climate-linked issues.

That's over ₹10 lakh crore - money that could've built hospitals, schools, infrastructure.

Instead, we'll spend it on damage control.

## What's Coming Next?

If we don't act, here's what Bharat 2035–2040 could look like:

- Heat-migration - families moving from cities to hills not for vacation, but survival
- Water rationing apps - where you bid for a 10-minute shower
- Children with daily medication for breathing and food allergies
- 24x7 mask-wearing society, not for COVID, but for air
- Housing societies building climate bunkers - with filters, cooling, and private borewells
- Food security warnings, even for the middle class
- Mental health breakdowns - anxiety, eco-grief, panic disorder becoming widespread

You may still have AC. You may still have a car.

But comfort doesn't protect you from collapse. Only resilience and action do.

## Final Wake-Up Call

You can dismiss a flood. You can survive a heatwave. You can filter bad water. You can even ignore a dead river.

But you cannot outrun a collapsing system.

And right now, every signal is blinking red.

This is not climate *change*. This is climate decay.

And Bharat isn't approaching the edge anymore.

We're already there.

## Coming Up Next:

Chapter 15: From Collapse to Comeback

From here, we shift gears. The next chapter begins the *solutions section* - the hopeful, actionable roadmap of how India can still turn the tide.

# PART II

## *The Comeback Begins*

# Chapter 15

# From Collapse to Comeback

*India's fightback begins with every citizen, every city, every step.*

If fear could fix the planet, we'd be saved by now.

But fear alone paralyses.

That's why this chapter - and every one after it - isn't just about sounding alarms. It's about picking up tools, lacing up shoes, planting roots, building back.

We're not too late.

Not yet.

## The Comeback Starts With Awareness - And Ownership

Change doesn't begin in a policy paper or a conference room. It begins in:

- A dust-choked street turned into a Sunday Green Run
- A school where children plant native trees instead of buying medals
- An apartment society that installs a compost pit instead of calling the garbage van
- An event professional who switches from vinyl banners to reusable branding
- A resident who says, "No more borewell drilling. Let's harvest rainwater."

When millions do small things, they start to move mountains.

## Green Runs, Loud Messages

In 2024, cities across India saw the rise of a new movement: Bharat Green Run.

- Neon-lit night marathons
- Tree plantation drives post-run
- Runners receiving seed medals, not plastic
- Pledge walls where people signed up to switch off ACs, reduce plastic, go vegan once a week
- Live music, sustainability stalls, children's storytelling corners - all powered by solar energy

These weren't just fitness events. They were public climate protests disguised as celebration.

Because not everyone reads climate reports. But everyone remembers a sweaty, euphoric run that made them feel like part of a cause.

## Cities That Lead the Way

The comeback will be city-led, or it won't happen at all.

Some examples already taking root:

- Indore: Ranked among the cleanest cities by involving citizens in composting and segregation
- Pune: Pushing for rooftop solar and water recycling in housing societies
- Bengaluru: Despite its chaos, now home to some of India's most active citizen water revival groups
- Delhi NCR: Urban farms on rooftops, RWAs banning single-use plastics, startups building air purification hubs

We need 100 Indores. 200 Punes. A billion aware citizens.

## The Personal Sustainability Checklist

Here's where you begin.

✅ Switch to a bamboo toothbrush

✅ Say no to single-use water bottles

✅ Install aerators on your taps – reduce water use by 50%

✅ Start composting – it's easier than you think

✅ Plant just 1 tree a month – and care for it

✅ Join or start a local Green Run in your city

✅ Cut meat consumption by 50% – or at least avoid red meat

✅ Refuse plastic bags. Carry a cloth one – every time

✅ Demand sustainability from the brands you buy

✅ Talk about the crisis. Normalize it in dinner table conversations

You don't have to do all. But start with one. And stay with it.

## Business, But Better

Events, corporates, housing societies - all play a role.

- Green Exhibitions with solar lights, recycled decor, digital invites
- Sustainable gifting using seeds, upcycled materials
- Eco-friendly conferences - zero-plastic zones, local catering, tree pledges
- Carbon offsets - every event pays for its emissions with plantation or solar sponsorships
- Waste audits - understand your mess, then clean it smarter

Sustainability doesn't mean stopping business.

It means doing business with brains and heart.

## Re-educate the Nation

Change the curriculum, change the country.

- Add climate science and sustainability to every schoolbook
- Make tree adoption, waste segregation, and energy use part of grading
- Celebrate eco-champions in local areas - not just actors or cricketers
- Run monthly climate sessions in every office, not just once a year

We trained India to compete.

Now we must train it to sustain.

## Hope Isn't Soft. It's a Weapon.

Hope is not passive.

Hope says:

- "I will stay and fight."
- "I will rebuild, replant, restore."
- "I will leave behind more trees than trash."

Because the opposite of collapse… isn't silence.

It's movement.

## This Is Just the Beginning...

This chapter was the spark.

But the fire? It's in:

- The next city's Green Run
- The next kid who tells their school to stop using thermocol
- The next society that bans borewell abuse
- The next office that decides "*no more plastic folders*"

The battle for Bharat 2035 isn't about saving polar bears.

It's about saving ourselves. And the comeback? It's already begun.

## Coming Up Next:

Chapter 16: The Greenprint for Bharat

A concrete, actionable, India-specific guide to building a sustainable future - from policy to pavement, classroom to corporate boardroom.

# Chapter 16

# The Greenprint for Bharat

*Not a dream. A design. Not a hope. A roadmap.*

We've warned.

We've wept.

We've watched things break.

Now, we build.

This isn't a utopian fantasy. It's a practical, people-powered greenprint to restore Bharat - from the top floors of glass towers to the roots of rural communities.

If we follow even half of it, 2035 won't be our endgame - it'll be our turning point.

## 1. Cities That Can Breathe

India is urbanizing fast - but if we keep building like we are, our cities will become death traps.

The Greenprint:

- Mandate urban tree cover of 33% in every city
- Make rooftop gardens, solar panels, and rainwater harvesting mandatory in new construction
- Convert one Sunday a month into Green Streets (no vehicles, open-air events, cycling, yoga)

- Designate Urban Cool Zones: public parks, water bodies, shaded corridors every 2 km
- Prioritize walkability and public transport over flyovers and signal-free corridors

Let's design cities for citizens, not just cars.

## 2. Water Smart, Not Water Desperate

India doesn't have a water shortage problem. It has a water mismanagement crisis.

The Greenprint:

- Install rainwater harvesting in every housing society
- Incentivize greywater reuse (for flushing, gardening)
- Enforce water metering for fair usage and billing
- Ban borewells in over-extracted zones – switch to community-managed tanks
- Protect and rejuvenate urban lakes, stepwells, and ponds

Water is not just for drinking. It's for living, growing, cooling, and thriving.

## 3. Clean the Air, Not Just Mask It

We cannot let the next generation grow up addicted to inhalers.

The Greenprint:

- Restrict diesel vehicles in metros by 2030
- Ban open burning of waste - and replace with community composting
- Convert all municipal vehicles to electric by 2028
- Mass plantation of native trees only - not decorative ones

- Equip schools and hospitals with indoor air purification systems powered by solar

Every breath matters. Design cities that don't kill us softly.

## 4. Sustainable Food for a Sustainable Future

Climate-friendly food isn't a trend. It's survival.

The Greenprint:

- Promote organic and regenerative farming - not chemical-heavy monoculture
- Invest in local food systems and farmers' markets
- Encourage school gardens - kids grow what they eat
- Offer tax breaks to food businesses that source sustainably
- Launch a "One Day Veg" campaign across corporates and campuses

If our food system collapses, nothing else matters.

## 5. Make Businesses Build Back Greener

The event industry, corporates, and real estate can be powerful allies - or reckless destroyers.

The Greenprint:

- Certify and rank green events - reward those that go zero-plastic and carbon neutral
- Offer subsidies for eco-friendly exhibition infrastructure (bamboo, fabric, LED, modular)
- Enforce ESG compliance - not just paperwork, but performance
- Promote green gifting in weddings, festivals, corporate promotions

- Turn every business conference into a platform for climate education as well

Sustainability isn't a cost. It's a competitive advantage.

## 6. Educate to Empower

If children aren't taught to protect the planet, they'll inherit a dying one.

The Greenprint:

- Integrate climate literacy in school curriculum by Class 3
- Launch Youth Climate Corps: high-schoolers earn credits through local green projects
- Make eco-habits part of report cards - composting, water use, plantation
- Encourage colleges to host Green Runs, Clean Drives, and Innovation Hackathons
- Every graduate must complete a 3-month sustainability internship - in farms, forests, or climate NGOs

We're not just raising children. We're raising first responders for Earth.

## 7. The Individual's Greenprint

Even without policy, you can be the greenprint in your colony, office, family.

Here's how:

- Stop chasing luxury, start embracing low-impact living
- Refuse plastic - even if it means inconvenience
- Switch to solar-powered appliances where possible

- Make zero-waste events a norm in your family
- Normalize second-hand and upcycled gifting
- Lead by example, not lectures

You don't need to do everything. But you must do something. Today.

## This Is Not a Sacrifice. It's an Upgrade.

Living sustainably doesn't mean living poorly. It means living smarter, longer, and with dignity.

We're not asking for less. We're asking for more of the right things:

- More trees
- More breathable air
- More clean water
- More real community
- More future to give our children

This isn't activism. This is architecting survival.

## Coming Up Next:

Chapter 17: The Climate Citizen

They aren't waiting for policy, applause, or perfection.

Just ordinary people taking extraordinary action - one compost bin, one cycle ride, one rooftop garden at a time.

# Chapter 17

# The Climate Citizen

*You don't need a title to lead the change.*

When we think of climate change, we think of glaciers melting, policies failing, or leaders speaking in air-conditioned halls.

What we don't often think of is a woman in Pune who composts every scrap of her kitchen waste.

Or a group of kids in Chennai who convinced their school to go plastic-free.

Or a delivery boy in Delhi who switched to an e-bike after his friend collapsed from heat exhaustion.

These are not activists. They're not influencers. They're climate citizens - ordinary people refusing to be bystanders in a crisis that affects them every day.

And in 2035, their stories might just save us all.

## The Power of One

"I'm just one person. What difference can I make?"

That question has killed more progress than any politician ever could.

Because change never starts with everyone. It starts with someone.

- Someone who says no to plastic cutlery

- Someone who fixes a leaky tap instead of ignoring it
- Someone who speaks up when a neighbor burns garbage
- Someone who refuses to wait for the government

Climate action doesn't always look like protests or speeches. Sometimes it looks like a terrace garden. A cycle ride. A metal straw.

And when one person changes, others watch. They learn. They copy. They multiply.

That's how revolutions begin.

## What Does It Mean To Be a Climate Citizen?

You don't need to quit your job, join a protest, or live in a forest.

You just need to start doing what's right - even when it's inconvenient.

Here's what it looks like:

1. ***Awareness***

Know where your water, food, and electricity come from. Track your household's waste, bills, and habits.

"I didn't even realize we were using 500 litres a day." – A resident of a Delhi high-rise, after installing a water meter

2. *Action*

Make small but consistent changes:

- Carry your own bottle, bag, and container
- Switch to LED lights and solar where possible
- Segregate your waste religiously
- Take public transport or carpool

3. *Advocacy*

You don't need a mic to have a voice.

- Talk about climate issues with friends and family
- Share verified facts on WhatsApp instead of fake forwards
- Organize a clean-up, a plantation drive, or a Green Run in your colony

## Real Stories, Real Change

**Komal, 34, Jaipur**

Started an "Eco Circle" in her apartment society. Now they compost, reuse greywater, and run a shared EV for errands.

**Ayaan, 12, Mumbai**

Convinced his school to switch from paper cups to steel tumblers. They now save over 30,000 cups a year.

**Ramesh, 29, Delhi**

Switched his Zomato delivery vehicle to an electric scooter. Saves ₹2,000 a month and breathes easier.

These aren't global news stories. They're our neighbours, classmates, and co-workers. They are the proof that you don't need permission to protect the planet.

## A 10-Step Climate Citizen Pledge

If you read nothing else in this chapter, read this.

Repeat it. Share it. Live it.

1. I will say NO to single-use plastic
2. I will fix water leaks and install tap aerators
3. I will compost my kitchen waste or find someone who will

4. I will use a cloth bag every single time I shop
5. I will switch off appliances when not in use
6. I will walk, cycle, or use public transport whenever possible
7. I will grow one plant every month
8. I will celebrate festivals without waste
9. I will talk about the climate crisis openly
10. I will act, even if no one else does

## Tools for the Modern Climate Citizen

You don't have to do it alone. Use technology to make it easier:

- JalTally - Tracks water usage per flat
- Recycle India - Find local collection centers for e-waste, plastic, clothes
- Good On You – Check if fashion brands are sustainable
- GrowIt - Gardening tips and community support for home growers
- Breathe India – Real-time AQI and suggestions for air purification

## Your Voice Matters

Don't underestimate the power of a phone call, a message, or a vote.

- Ask your local grocery store to stop using plastic
- Tell your RWA to install rainwater harvesting
- Message your MLA to push for air monitoring stations in your area

- Write reviews praising eco-friendly businesses

Change happens when silence ends.

## From Consumer to Creator

You are not just a user. You're a builder of the future.

Everything you do - or don't do - shapes the air your children breathe, the water they drink, the land they walk on.

Being a climate citizen is not a trend. It's not a burden. It's a badge of courage.

And in Bharat 2035, courage is our only currency.

## Coming Up Next:

Chapter 18: The Rise of Green Business

How sustainability is becoming India's next big industry - and why the companies that don't adapt will vanish with the old world.

# Chapter 18

# The Rise of Green Business

*If your business isn't sustainable, it's not future-proof.*

For decades, business in India meant one thing: scale. Bigger factories. Bigger profits. Bigger footprints.

But something changed.

The floods came. The water ran out. The air became unbreathable. And customers - especially the younger ones - started asking:

"What is your brand doing for the planet?"

In Bharat 2035, the companies that survive aren't the ones with the biggest ads. They're the ones with the smallest carbon footprints.

Welcome to the age of green business - where doing good is no longer a CSR activity. It's core strategy.

## Why Green Business Is Booming in India

The old logic was: sustainability is expensive.

The new truth is: climate collapse is unaffordable.

- Cities face 3–5 power cuts a week due to heat-related demand
- Events are cancelled due to pollution spikes
- Raw materials are disrupted by floods and droughts

- Consumers are dropping brands they no longer trust

And the data agrees:

A 2024 Nielsen India report found that 71% of Indian Gen Z buyers prefer eco-conscious brands - even if they cost more.

Over ₹18,000 crore of ESG-focused mutual funds were launched in India in 2023 alone.

Green business isn't a niche anymore. It's the new market.

## Startups That Are Saving the Future

Some of India's most exciting new ventures aren't making apps - they're making impact.

***Attero Recycling – Noida***

Turns e-waste into raw materials like copper, gold, lithium. India's first lithium battery recycler.

***Beco – Mumbai***

Sells biodegradable home & kitchen products. From bamboo tissues to compostable garbage bags.

***Bare Necessities – Bengaluru***

Zero-waste personal care products - packaging-free and refillable.

Run primarily by women.

***Yulu – Pan-India***

Electric bike-sharing that reduces traffic and pollution in metros. Used by delivery giants and office workers alike.

These aren't just businesses. They're blueprints.

## Events, Exhibitions, and Eco-Innovation

The event industry - once waste-heavy - is transforming too.

Green-minded organizers now use:

- Fabric backdrops instead of vinyl
- Modular, reusable stall designs
- LED lighting powered by solar generators
- Digital brochures and QR-based info displays

Some even offer carbon-neutral weddings, where every guest's carbon footprint is offset by tree planting or rural solar donation.

Clients no longer just want fancy. They want future-ready.

## Big Brands, Bigger Shifts

Even India's biggest names are adapting:

- Tata Group pledged net-zero by 2045 across all verticals
- ITC became plastic neutral - collecting more than it sells
- Zomato now highlights eco-friendly packaging on its platform
- Reliance launched recycled polyester under its R|Elan range

And here's the twist - they're not doing it out of guilt. They're doing it for competitive survival.

Because the old ways? They're getting taxed, banned, or boycotted.

## Green Is Not a Cost - It's an Opportunity

5 Fast-Growing Green Sectors in India:

1. Renewable Energy

   Solar, wind, biofuel - already a ₹3 lakh crore+ industry

2. EV and Battery Tech

   India aims for 30% EVs by 2030. Massive growth in charging infra & battery swapping

3. Sustainable Packaging

   From banana-leaf plates to mushroom-based styrofoam alternatives

4. Organic and Regenerative Farming

   Supported by both government subsidies and urban demand

5. Climate-Tech & AI for Sustainability

   Startups using IoT, drones, and AI to monitor water use, crop health, and carbon emissions

Green = Growth. Period.

## Green Business in Tier 2 & 3 Cities

This isn't just a metro trend.

In Indore, waste-to-compost startups are booming. In Ludhiana, fabric manufacturers are switching to plant-based dyes. In Surat, solar installations are powering entire diamond factories.

Climate entrepreneurship is the next wave of Make in India.

And guess what?

It's not elite. It's inclusive.

## Brands That Refused to Adapt

Let's be honest - some businesses didn't get the memo.

- Single-use plastic brands banned from export
- Old-style fashion chains called out for water-wasting dyes
- Luxury builders fined for illegal borewells and heat-trap designs

These are not failures of commerce. They're failures of foresight.

## Building a Green Business? Ask These 5 Questions:

1. Is your product necessary, or just another landfill filler?
2. Can you reuse, recycle, or reduce your input?
3. Are you treating waste as raw material?
4. Is your workforce trained for climate resilience?
5. Are you solving a real climate pain point, or greenwashing?

The future belongs to those who answer these honestly.

## 2035: What Will Thrive?

- Flea markets of upcycled fashion
- Carbon-negative cafes in tech parks
- Event agencies that plant trees instead of handing swag bags
- Solar-powered ghost kitchens with zero plastic output
- Hyperlocal brands with zero delivery emissions

In Bharat 2035, the businesses that last are the ones that heal while they grow.

Because people aren't just buying stuff anymore.

They're buying impact.

## Coming Up Next:

Chapter 19: Cities of Tomorrow

From rooftop farms to zero-waste apartments - a practical blueprint for transforming Indian cities into climate-safe zones.

# Chapter 19

# Cities of Tomorrow

*Not built on concrete. Built on courage, common sense, and community.*

In 2023, India's cities felt like pressure cookers. No water in the taps. No clean air. Flooded roads. Melting tar. Garbage burning in landfills.

And yet, millions moved in each year - chasing dreams, jobs, and hope.

But hope needs habitat. And Bharat 2035 cannot survive inside cities built for a climate that no longer exists.

It's time to ask:

What should a real Indian city look like in the age of climate collapse?

Because the cities of tomorrow aren't in space. They're here - waiting to be designed better.

## The Truth About Urban India Today

- Over 35% of India's population lives in cities - expected to cross 50% by 2040
- 21 of the world's 30 most polluted cities are Indian
- 7 out of 10 Indian cities are already at risk of extreme heat, water shortage, or flooding
- But only a handful are actively preparing for the crisis

We're building vertical towers on dying rivers. Malls on drained wetlands. Flyovers while the air chokes underneath.

If that's our smart city - we're heading for a very dumb future.

## The Anatomy of a Climate-Ready City

A city that survives - and thrives - in 2035 must have:

1. ***Breathable Air Zones***

- Tree cover of at least 30%
- Strict emission control on diesel and construction
- Vertical gardens on building facades
- EV-only lanes in key zones

2. ***Water Resilience***

- Rainwater harvesting in every building
- Lakes revived as community water banks
- Greywater used for flushing/gardening
- Monthly water audits by RWAs

3. ***Heat Management***

- "Cool roofs" - painted white or tiled with reflective materials
- Urban Cool Corridors: shaded pedestrian + cycle paths every 1.5 km
- Mandated tree planting along every 100 meters of road

4. ***Waste to Resource Thinking***

- Zero-landfill policies for housing societies
- Mandatory segregation, composting, and e-waste collection

- Community biogas units in residential zones

*5. Mobility with Brains*

- Non-motorized transport lanes
- Electric bus fleets and last-mile green shuttles
- Incentives for car-free days

## Cities That Are Already Leading

*Indore*

India's cleanest city five years in a row – because it treats cleanliness like a religion.

Community composting units, street-level segregation, and awareness drives by kids.

*Chennai*

Post-2019 drought, the city began reviving old lakes and stepwells. The restoration of Retteri Lake now supplies water to 2 lakh homes.

*Pune*

Over 300 km of dedicated cycling tracks planned. Rainwater harvesting mandatory in new construction.

*Surat*

Solar panels on municipal buildings. Flood-resilient infrastructure built after the 2006 disaster now used as a model globally.

These are not perfect cities. But they're trying - and that alone sets them apart.

## Greener Buildings, Smarter Blocks

If buildings are the bones of a city, we need to redesign the skeleton.

A 2035-ready building will have:

- Solar panels and battery backups
- Smart water meters and leak sensors
- Compost pits and organic gardens
- Reflective rooftops to reduce urban heat
- Shared EV charging stations in basements

And they won't just be in gated societies. They'll be in government housing, offices, colleges, and temples.

Because everyone deserves a future - not just the wealthy.

## The Forgotten Infrastructure: Emotion and Access

Climate-smart doesn't mean sterile. It means humane.

Cities of Tomorrow will also have:

- Public benches under trees, not under billboards
- Community libraries made of recycled material
- Repair cafes where broken items are fixed, not thrown
- Water ATMs at every metro station, not just malls
- Solar-powered street vendors, not just solar factories

These little things? They build connection, dignity, and resilience.

## What You Can Do in Your City

Whether you're a tenant, builder, or business - here's what action looks like:

*RWAs:*

- Install rainwater harvesting.
- Ban thermocol in events.
- Run composting workshops.

*Offices:*

- Switch to digital ID cards and e-bills.
- Incentivize public transport or carpooling.
- Ban plastic bottles from meetings.

*Schools:*

- Assign trees to students.
- Host monthly zero-waste days.
- Run climate clubs with local action projects.

*Businesses:*

- Use cloth/fiber bags.
- Offer discount for container-carrying customers.
- Join or sponsor a Green Run in your city.

## What 2035 Could Look Like (If We Get It Right)

- Rooftop farms growing food in every colony
- Waste-to-energy units powering streetlights
- Kids walking to school under shaded green corridors
- Festivals with seed-packets, not plastic return gifts

- No diesel autos. No illegal borewells. No garbage mountains.

India doesn't need futuristic sci-fi cities. We need resilient, breathable, inclusive cities - made not by tech, but by heart.

## This Is the India We Deserve

We've all seen what doesn't work. Broken drains. Burnt fields. Concrete deserts.

Let's now build what does.

Not tomorrow. Not when it's funded. Now.

Because when the climate knocks on your door, it won't ask your designation. It'll ask - Did you act?

## Coming Up Next:

Chapter 20: Reclaiming the Everyday

Big change doesn't always begin in boardrooms or city halls.

Sometimes, it starts with a dustbin — and a decision to do things differently, every single day.

# Chapter 20

# Reclaiming the Everyday

*Change doesn't begin in boardrooms. It begins at breakfast*

You don't need to save the planet. You just need to stop helping destroy it.

We keep waiting for the big fix. A new law. A tech breakthrough. A government scheme.

But Bharat won't be saved in Parliament. It will be saved in your kitchen. Your balcony. Your society WhatsApp group. Your child's lunchbox.

Because the comeback begins in the smallest of places - the ones we ignore.

This chapter isn't about idealism. It's about reality. How reclaiming simple, everyday choices can collectively reverse the climate collapse that's already begun.

We're not too late. But we're down to the wire.

## The Climate Crisis Begins at Home

Not in the rainforest. Not at COP28.

Right here:

- In the garbage you toss out mixed with food waste
- In the 30-minute shower you took "to relax"
- In the 14 online deliveries you made this week

- In the 7 sachets, 3 tissue wraps, and 1 takeout box from dinner last night

We've normalized destruction - in the name of lifestyle. And now, it's time to normalize survival.

## Segregation Isn't "Good Citizenship" - It's Non-Negotiable

Every time we mix wet and dry waste, we:

- Ruin recyclables
- Create methane bombs in landfills
- Force sanitation workers to inhale poison

India generates over 62 million tonnes of waste annually - most of it unsegregated.

✓ Start with 3 bins: wet, dry, and rejects

✓ Put signage. Educate your staff. Involve your kids.

✓ No plastic in compost. No food in plastic. No excuses.

Don't wait for a "clean-up drive." Your bin is the battlefield.

## Compost: From Stink to Solution

40% of Indian household waste is organic. Most of it goes to landfills - where it releases methane, a greenhouse gas 84x more potent than $CO_2$.

But here's the fix - it's called home composting.

- Small bins available online or at local nurseries
- No smell if done right. No insects. No drama.
- In 3–4 weeks: fresh, earthy compost that can enrich plants or community gardens

*One apartment can reduce 500–700 kg of landfill waste per year - just by composting.*

That's not climate action. That's basic hygiene.

## Reclaiming Water: One Drop at a Time

We don't need fancy gadgets or high-end filters to save water.

We need:

- Tap aerators that cut usage by 40–60%
- Buckets over showers
- Reuse of RO waste for mopping, flushing
- Rainwater harvesting tanks in every building
- Borewell bans in over-extracted zones

In Bengaluru, some RWAs now reuse 90% of their greywater. In Chennai, tankers charge ₹2,000 a trip during summer - forcing societies to retrofit rain tanks.

Water isn't just precious. It's political.

And unless we reclaim control, we'll be paying for it like gold.

## The Cloth Bag Isn't a Symbol. It's a Statement.

Still asking, "Sir, ek carry bag milega?" We've failed.

Plastic bags are banned in many states - and still used everywhere.

Reality check:

- A single plastic bag takes 500–1,000 years to degrade
- India uses over 13 million tonnes of plastic annually - and recycles less than 60%

What you can do:

- Carry a cloth bag – always
- Say no at checkout. Even if it's awkward.
- Refuse single-use plastic spoons, straws, and plates - especially at events and takeaways

*Your tote bag isn't old-school. It's survival gear.*

## The Return of the Balcony Garden

You don't need a farm.

You need 4 pots. 3 hours. And some sunlight.

Grow:

- Lemongrass, tulsi, mint - herbs that clean air and support bees
- Tomatoes, spinach, chillies - in 6–8 weeks
- Vertical greens using recycled bottles or wall planters

  Benefits?

- Food security. Pollution control. Mental well-being.
- And a tiny rebellion against food miles and pesticide-packed sabzi

*One woman in Pune grows 70% of her kitchen herbs on a 2×4 ft balcony.*

This isn't luxury. This is modern resistance.

## The Climate Ride to the Kirana

You don't need an EV to fight emissions.

- Walk for short errands
- Cycle for groceries

- Club 3 tasks into one drive
- Switch off your engine at signals (saves fuel + cuts fumes)
- Encourage your RWA to build cycle stands or partner with rental startups

The less you drive, the more we survive.

You're not just burning petrol. You're burning time, air, and sanity.

## Real People. Real Change.

**Radhika, 58, Gurugram:** Installed composters in her society. They now divert 100 kg of waste weekly.

**Gaurav, 31, Bengaluru:** Built a community tool library - neighbours now borrow instead of buying.

**Amal, 42, Chennai:** Set up a rainwater recharge pit in his colony. The borewell hasn't dried in 2 years.

**Lata, 23, Mumbai:** Runs Instagram workshops on balcony gardening - has taught over 1,000 people.

**Shalabh, 45, Delhi:** Installed aerators, planted 15 trees, and banned plastic bottles from his kid's birthday parties.

They didn't protest. They planted. Fixed. Segregated. Reused.

They didn't change the world. They changed their part of it.

## Your Family Is a Climate Team

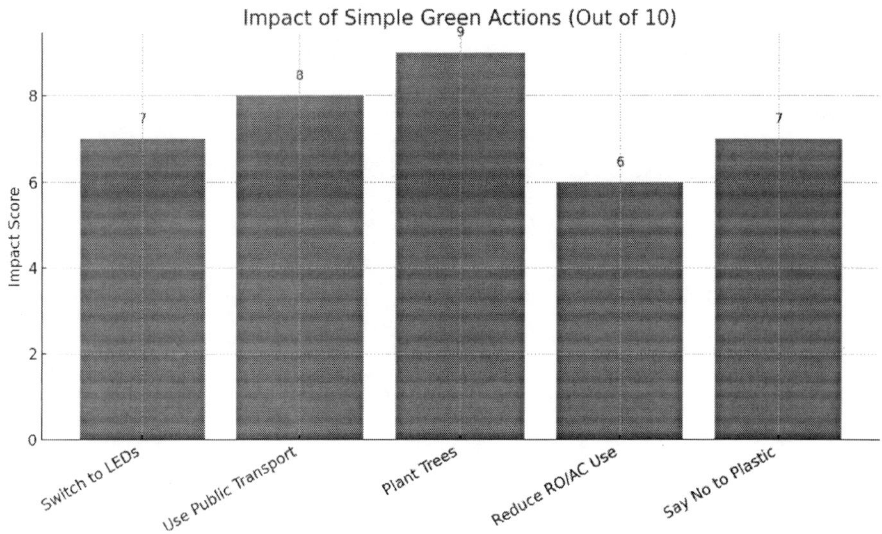


Assign green roles:

- Kids: water plants, clean up wrappers, say no to plastic
- Parents: track electricity, install low-flow taps, compost
- Grandparents: educate helpers, reuse containers, monitor leaks

Run "green audits" at home:

- How much plastic did we throw?
- How many deliveries this month?
- How much water was wasted?

Make sustainability a team game - not a punishment.

This Isn't a Trend. It's a Reclaiming.

We didn't always live this way.

Our parents:

- Reused jars, carried cloth bags, repaired things, cooked at home
- Had backyard trees, terrace tanks, and no air conditioning

We called it old-fashioned. Now we call it sustainable.

We don't need new habits. We just need to remember the ones we forgot.

## Final Words: The War Starts at Home

The planet doesn't need saviours. It needs *participants.*

If your building segregates waste, that's climate action. If your child carries a metal bottle, that's climate action. If you turn off the tap while brushing, that's climate action.

And if millions do it together - collapse becomes comeback.

Right now, every home is a climate battlefield. And survival... is a routine.

## Coming Up Next:

Chapter 21: Cities That Heal Instead of Hurt

Our cities weren't designed to save us. But they still can.

From vertical forests to floodproof lakes, this chapter explores how Indian cities - with the right vision and will - can go from heat islands to hope zones.

# Chapter 21

# Cities That Heal Instead of Hurt

*How Indian Cities Can Regenerate, Not Just Survive*

What we build decides whether we live, or merely survive.

We thought our cities would give us progress. Opportunity. Development. A better life.

But what they gave us instead was:

- 3-hour traffic jams

- 48-degree summers

- Broken drains, choking smog, plastic-filled rivers

- And the quiet panic of wondering if our kids will ever see a blue sky again

This wasn't a design flaw. This was the design.

Because we built our cities to grow. Not to breathe.

## India's Urban Explosion - A Ticking Time Bomb

- By 2035, over 600 million Indians will live in cities
- 70% of India's GDP comes from urban areas - but so does 80% of its emissions
- Our cities occupy just 3% of land, but generate over 60% of pollution
- Delhi, Mumbai, Bengaluru, and Kolkata are all projected to become unlivable heat zones by 2050

And yet, what do we keep building?

⊘ Cement towers

⊘ Flyovers

⊘ Malls

⊘ Gated societies with no trees

⊘ Roads that flood the second it rains

We don't have cities. We have urban furnaces.

## Cities Are Now Cooking Their Citizens

- Urban heat island effect = cities are 4-7°C hotter than rural areas
- Heat gets trapped in concrete, glass, and asphalt - and there's no green cover to cool it
- ACs dump hot air into the streets, making it worse
- Pavement heat can reach 60-70°C in peak summer

And we keep wondering why:

- Pedestrians collapse
- Birds fall from the sky
- Car dashboards melt
- Kids get nosebleeds in May

We didn't inherit this heat. We manufactured it.

## The Green is Gone. So is the Oxygen.

Every city master plan has a joke printed in it: "green buffer zone" What is that now?

- A mall.

- A wedding lawn.
- A garbage dump.

We've lost:

- 80% of trees in Bengaluru in 40 years
- 75% of lakes in Hyderabad
- 65% of Delhi's forested area to "development"

Without trees, there's:

- No cooling
- No air purification
- No birdlife
- No soul

We made our cities smarter. And stripped them of wisdom.

## But What If Cities Could Heal?

Imagine this:

- Streets lined with neem, peepal, and amaltas
- Rooftops growing spinach, tomatoes, and tulsi
- Lakes cleaned, revived, and reconnected to ground recharge
- Walkable zones with no cars - just people, cycles, fresh air
- Offices using natural light, solar energy, and rainwater harvesting
- Metro rides replacing 500 cars a day
- Schools composting, greening, and teaching real climate education

Sounds utopian?

Cities across India are already doing it.

## Real Stories, Real Hope

**Indore**
- Named India's cleanest city multiple times

- Aggressive waste segregation, decentralized composting

- 100+ urban gardens from reclaimed dumping grounds

**Surat**
- Zero-waste textile units

- Riverfront reclaimed for green zones

- Climate-resilient infrastructure post-1994 plague

**Pune**
- 1,200+ housing societies composting

- Active citizen groups driving lake clean-ups

- Pune Metro integrated with cycling tracks

**Chennai**
- Restored 210 water bodies

- Raised over 100 urban forests through Miyawaki method

- Rooftop farming pilot projects in low-income areas

These aren't PR stunts. These are urban revolutions - just not on the front page.

## The Future Isn't Flyovers. It's Footpaths.

Every time we build a flyover, we destroy:

- A neighbourhood
- A water drain
- A tree line

- A walkable alternative

Instead, we need:

- Shaded pavements
- Public transport networks that *work*
- Cycle highways like the ones in the Netherlands
- Parking caps, not parking towers

If a city isn't walkable, it isn't livable. Mobility isn't about speed. It's about *dignity.*

## Urban Planning = Climate Planning

We cannot talk about climate change without talking about:

- Drainage systems
- Zoning laws
- Construction materials
- Tree cover
- Public transport access

Cities must be redesigned with:

- Green Building Codes - mandatory rooftop solar, thermal insulation, waste treatment
- Flood Maps - prevent illegal construction on low-lying or natural floodplains
- Urban Forest Mandates - every new project must create canopy cover
- Water Neutrality Goals - buildings must recharge more water than they consume

Planning isn't paperwork. It's survival protocol.

## Building Cities That Breathe

Start small. In your own locality:

- Identify spots for micro forests (unused plots, corners, roundabouts)
- Use Miyawaki technique - dense, fast-growing native trees
- Involve schoolkids, elders, shopkeepers - build ownership
- Run tree audit campaigns - map, label, and protect old trees

Create:

- Green corridors connecting parks and tree clusters
- Rain gardens to catch water runoff
- Community chill zones with shaded benches and mist fans

These aren't fancy ideas. These are *heatwave insurance.*

## Builders, Architects, Authorities - Your Move

A message to the people shaping cities:

- Don't build another glass box that needs ACs to survive
- Don't flatten a tree for parking
- Don't design gated societies that ignore the street outside
- Don't price out the poor from green spaces

Design for life. Not just for rent yield.

Your blueprint is a breathing document. Treat it like lungs.

## For the People. By the People.

City change doesn't have to wait for government budgets.

Look at:

- Citizen clean-up groups in Mumbai reviving beaches and drains
- Rainwater activists in Hyderabad turning apartments into recharge stations
- Lake warriors in Bengaluru mapping pollution, filing PILs, and winning
- Tree census volunteers in Gurugram tagging every tree under threat

These aren't urban activists. These are urban parents. Grandparents. Teachers. Plumbers. Coders. Children.

They're not fixing the city. They're reclaiming it.

## Final Words: Build Like We Want to Stay

We always thought the goal was to build more. Taller. Faster. Shinier.

Now we know: If we build wrong - we burn.

The cities we create today will decide whether:

- Children breathe with lungs or with inhalers
- Lakes survive or turn to concrete dumps
- Summers are endured or escaped
- Birds sing or disappear forever

We can either build heat islands... Or healing zones.

We can keep designing for profit. Or we can finally start designing for life.

## Coming Up Next:

Chapter 22: Business, But Greener

The future won't belong to the biggest brands, it'll belong to the most responsible ones.

From stall designers to startups, it's not about following the green revolution, it's about leading it.

# Chapter 22

# Business, But Greener

*If they're the future, why aren't we protecting it?*

Sustainability isn't a CSR checkbox anymore. It's your business model now.

For decades, we've measured business success in rupees, reach, and returns.

But in Bharat 2035, there's a new metric rising fast: Regret.

Regret from brands that ignored the signs. From industries that chased scale, not sense. From events that generated applause – and 4 tonnes of garbage. From businesses that polluted rivers for profit, only to drown in public backlash later.

This isn't guilt-tripping. This is the market now.

And if your business isn't going green - it's already going obsolete.

## Why Business as Usual Is Now a Liability

Let's be brutally honest. Traditional business practices in India are:

- Resource-hungry
- Waste-generating
- Carbon-heavy

- Emotionally disconnected from community impact

Consider this:

- The events industry in India generates over 100,000 tonnes of waste per year, much of it non-recyclable
- Textile factories in Tiruppur dump untreated dye water directly into rivers
- Exhibition stalls use synthetic boards, flex banners, and plastic décor — often discarded after 3 days
- Delivery companies run massive fleets with zero climate accountability

Every transaction now leaves a trail: Carbon, packaging, wastewater, landfill space.

And your customer is watching.

## The Indian Consumer Is Waking Up

India's younger population - 65% under 35 - is more aware, anxious, and climate-conscious than ever.

They now ask:

- "Is this product cruelty-free?"
- "Did this brand support sustainability, or just sell it?"
- "Is this event zero-waste or greenwashed?"

❢ 78% of Gen Z in India say they're willing to pay more for sustainable products

❢ Brands like Bare Necessities, The Better India Store, Farmerr, and Bhoomi are winning loyal followings by putting planet before packaging

They don't want perfection. They want honesty.

And that's now your strongest currency.

## Green Business Is Smart Business

Here's what happens when you go green:

- Lower costs (less packaging, better efficiency, reduced energy bills)
- Greater brand love (eco-conscious buyers = loyal communities)
- Future-proofing (against environmental regulations and supply shocks)
- Investor interest (ESG funds are booming globally)

Sustainability is no longer a PR play. It's a profit strategy.

Not convinced?

Look at:

- ITC - Recycled over 99% of solid waste; now a benchmark in circular business
- Zerodha - Solar-powered HQ, minimalist operations, paperless by default
- Marriott India - Banned single-use plastic bottles from 80+ hotels
- IKEA - Committed ₹3,000 crore in India for sustainable retail practices

These aren't side efforts. They're central missions.

## The Green Shift in Events & Exhibitions

If you're in the business of experience - events, exhibitions, activations - the transformation is urgent.

What needs to go:

- Foam boards, flex banners, plastic décor
- Single-use props, disposable water bottles
- Generator-fueled lights, diesel-powered structures

What needs to come in:

- Eco boards (recyclable panels)
- Digital displays (reuse and update instead of print)
- Solar energy or hybrid power support
- Modular stall design (for reuse)
- On-site waste segregation and composting
- Sustainable gifting (plantable kits, local crafts, edible items)

One standout example is **Happy & Hungry – The Event Co.**, a new-age event company quietly leading India's transition toward greener experiences. From eco-stall fabrication and zero-waste corporate events to digital entry systems and sustainable gifting, they've proven that you don't need to choose between visual impact and environmental responsibility.

Imagine an exhibition where:

- Every stall is recyclable
- Every visitor carries a digital pass
- Every vendor follows a zero-waste pledge

That's not the future. That's the new standard.

## For Startups and D2C Brands: Lead the Way

Startups are perfectly positioned to embed sustainability from day one.

Ways to do it:

- Choose biodegradable packaging or recycled materials
- Source locally to reduce emissions and build community trust
- Audit your energy, water, and material consumption
- Use green certifications (like FSC, Ecomark, GOTS) where possible
- Tell your climate story - not just what you sell, but *why* you're different

💡 Bonus: Eco-conscious branding attracts press, influencers, and grants.

Your impact is your USP now.

## For Corporates: Go Beyond CSR

No one reads the fine print of a glossy CSR report anymore.

They see:

- How your factories treat rivers
- How your delivery network handles emissions
- Whether your boardroom uses AC at 18°C in December

Real climate leadership means:

- Divesting from fossil-heavy partnerships
- Moving fleets to electric
- Setting hard targets (e.g., carbon neutral by 2035)

- Tying leadership bonuses to sustainability metrics
- Partnering with climate NGOs for measurable ground work

It's not about marketing. It's about modeling the future.

## Mindset Shift: From Profit-Only to Planet-Proof

Ask:

- What does my product leave behind after use?
- Can this process be done with less water, less energy, less plastic?
- Am I solving a real problem - or just selling more stuff?

If you're in:

- Retail → Offer refill stations, discounts for reusing packaging
- Food → Source from sustainable farms, ban plastic cutlery
- Events → Switch to QR-based entries, eco gift bags, green vendors
- Services → Go paperless, run carbon-neutral campaigns, plant for every sale
- Construction → Use fly ash bricks, local stone, natural lighting

It's not about shutting shop. It's about cleaning it up.

## The Green Advantage in Hiring, Funding & Reputation

You'll notice:

- Young talent prefers mission-driven companies
- ESG investors demand clean practices

- Global partners ask for your environmental impact reports
- Awards and certifications now heavily favor sustainable innovations

Being green is no longer niche. It's competitive advantage.

Build that story now - or be left out of tomorrow's economy.

## Final Words: Build the Business That Makes You Proud

In 2035, your business will be asked just one thing:

"Did you help fix the problem - or profit from it?"

Be the stall fabricator that pioneered reusable booths. Be the D2C brand that banned bubble wrap. Be the event company — like Happy & Hungry – The Event Co. - that proved zero-waste is not only possible, but profitable. Be the startup that said: *we can do well by doing good.*

Because the truth is:

- Customers will remember the brands that cared
- Investors will reward the ones that adapted
- And the planet will only spare the ones that changed

Sustainability is no longer the side dish. It's the main business plan.

## Coming Up Next:

Chapter 23: Children of Change

Why India's greatest hope lies in the smallest voices — and how Gen Z is already leading the sustainability revolution.

# Chapter 23

# Children of Change

*They didn't create the mess. But they're cleaning it up anyway.*

Every evening in Noida, Ayaan, age 11, waters two neem saplings near the society gate.

His schoolmate, Advika runs a "No Plastic Pouch" campaign on her street. She's 12.

In Chennai, Zoya, age 9, refuses to celebrate her birthday with balloons -"They harm birds," she says.

They didn't attend COP summits. They didn't draft any policies. They don't even have voting rights.

And yet — they are acting like leaders in a crisis that adults are still arguing about.

Welcome to India's Generation Z+, the children of change.

## They Were Born Into a Burning World

- They've never known a winter without smog
- They can't drink tap water
- They have memories of floods, power cuts, and water queues
- They've inhaled more PM2.5 than their grandparents did in a lifetime

But instead of despairing, they are doing.

Because for them, this isn't about saving the planet someday. It's about surviving today.

## The Classroom Is the New Climate Ground Zero

More and more schools in India are waking up to reality:

"If we don't teach climate in Class 3, we'll be teaching survival skills in Class 10."

That's why schools in Bengaluru, Ahmedabad, and Mumbai are now:

- Running weekly *eco clubs*
- Assigning *trees instead of trophies*
- Hosting *Green Fairs* and *Compost Challenges*
- Teaching students to track their *carbon footprints* alongside math homework

And guess what?

The kids love it.

They're not lazy. They're not distracted. They're just waiting to be trusted.

## Child-Led Movements That Inspired Adults

### Clean My India - *Indore*

Started by 6th graders after a garbage dump appeared near their colony. They wrote to the municipal officer, petitioned with signatures, and got it cleaned.

### Paint the Dustbin - *Pune*

Teens painted community bins with flowers, slogans, and climate facts — to make waste sorting cool.

**No-Pack Lunch Days – *Hyderabad***

Children started bringing steel lunchboxes wrapped in cloth, and inspired teachers and canteen staff to ditch disposables.

These aren't exceptions. They're precedents.

## Kids Who Changed Homes

It's not just what they do at school. It's how they change what happens at home.

Parents across India now report:

- "My son refuses to let us use plastic straws."
- "My daughter switches off lights if we leave them on."
- "Our family installed a compost bin — all because of a school project."

Children are the smallest negotiators with the biggest emotional influence. And once they understand climate... they don't forget.

They nag. They question. They push. Until change becomes habit.

## How Schools Can Shape Climate Citizens

Every school in India — rural, urban, big, or small — can start with:

✅ A native tree planted per student per year

✅ A rainwater harvesting demo unit

✅ Compost pits in school kitchens

✅ Climate storytelling sessions (in local languages too!)

✅ Annual "Green Report Card" — tracking real change, not just exams

This isn't extra work. This is the work that matters most.

## Beyond Textbooks: Hands-On Climate Skills

Let's raise children who can:

- Grow their own herbs
- Segregate their waste
- Understand what a heatwave means for their health
- Speak up when a borewell is dug illegally
- Choose a product based on its packaging, not just branding

Because awareness without action is anxiety. We owe them the tools, not just the truth.

## What India's Future Could Look Like — If They Lead

- Colleges with climate entrepreneurship clubs
- Children's Green Parliaments in every state
- Eco-internships in farms, forests, and clean-tech startups
- Young eco-podcasters, bloggers, and coders influencing millions
- City councils inviting teen delegates to co-design public spaces

We don't need saviors. We need enablers — parents, teachers, corporates — who let them lead.

Because if they can design our apps... they can design our survival too.

## The Real Revolution Has No Beards or Suits

They may not write manifestos. They may not trend on Twitter. But they are watching. Learning. Acting.

And in their quiet choices - skipping balloons, refusing plastic, planting trees - India's real climate revolution is growing.

These children won't wait for us. They'll grow their own way.

Let's not slow them down.

Let's hand them tools, not trauma.

Because they're not just children of change.

They are the change.

## Afterword: Bharat 2035 – The Comeback We Can Still Create

A poetic, powerful conclusion imagining what Bharat 2035 could still become - not a disaster, but a defining moment of collective courage and recovery.

# The Last Page Is Yours

This book warned of what Bharat could become by 2035 if we stay silent. But this closing vision is not of disaster – it's of redemption. Because if we act now, 2035 won't be the year it all ended. It will be the year we turned the tide.

The ink isn't dry. The ending isn't fixed. The story is still in your hands.

If you've reached this point, you already know the truth: Bharat is burning. Choking. Drowning. Disappearing. And yet – it's still breathing. That breath? It's you.

This book has told you stories of heatstroke, polluted skies, dry taps, and silent forests. It has shown you collapsing systems, compounding crises, and irreversible tipping points. But it has also shown you something else. Choice. The choice to give up or grow green. To watch the world break or to step forward and rebuild it.

**This Isn't About Climate. It's About Courage. Courage to:** • Speak when everyone is silent • Change when it's inconvenient • Plant when you may never see the tree fully grown • Raise children to be warriors of the earth, not just survivors • Host events, build homes, and run businesses that do less harm and more healing You are not too small. You are not too late. You are not alone.

**The First Step Already Exists It could be:** • A Green Run you join • A child you mentor in climate education • A rooftop garden you build • A society meeting where you raise your voice • A compost bin, a bucket, a steel bottle, a solar light The tools are everywhere. The question is: will you pick them up?

**One Day,** They'll Ask Your children. Your grandkids. Your younger siblings. They'll ask: "When the forests were burning… what did you do?" "When the rivers ran dry… did you act?" "When Bharat stood at the edge… did you just scroll past the headlines?" And you — if you've read this far, you'll have an answer. "I didn't wait. I stood up. I did something. I began the comeback."

**The Final Chapter Was Never Meant to Be Written By Me It's meant to be written by:** • The young event planner who turns her first big client into a zero-waste success story • The father who plants trees for his daughter's 10th birthday instead of balloons • The building secretary who bans plastic in all society functions • The runner who turns a marathon into a movement • The teenager who becomes the reason her school gets solar panels I wrote the chapters. But this page? That belongs to you.

**Bharat 2035 Can Still Be Beautiful Not perfect**. Not painless. But survivable. Livable. Green. Real. Human. And if we're lucky — healing. Because the last page is not a period. It's a pen. And it's in your hands now.

**The End. Or maybe… The Beginning.**

# Acknowledgements

Writing this book was not just a creative effort - it was an emotional one. A response to the suffering I witnessed, the helplessness I felt, and the fierce urgency to act.

First and foremost, I want to thank the countless unnamed citizens of India - guards, workers, students, mothers, teachers, and children - whose daily struggles and small acts of courage inspired many chapters in this book. You are the real climate warriors.

To my parents & wife Radhika - thank you for giving me the space, strength, and late-night chai breaks that helped me stay grounded while writing about such heavy truths.

To the friends who challenged my drafts, pushed me to go deeper, and reminded me to keep the tone human - I am forever grateful.

This book was born the day I saw a man collapse from heat in front of my eyes - and chose not to look away. To that guard, whose name I never got, I owe more than words. Your death sparked this journey, and I promise it will not go in vain.

And finally, to every reader holding this book: thank you for caring. For feeling. For not scrolling past. You are part of this fight now - and I believe, truly, that we still have time to win.

**- Mudit Jain**

# Legal Disclaimer

This book is a work of non-fiction based on publicly available information, real-life events, journalistic sources, and credible scientific research. Every effort has been made to ensure accuracy, authenticity, and responsible reporting.

The content reflects the author's analysis, interpretation, and perspective on environmental, social, and infrastructural issues affecting India. The statistics, data points, and studies referenced in this book have been sourced from government reports, peer-reviewed publications, environmental NGOs, and reputable media houses. Where available, citations have been provided.

Any references to brands, institutions, services, or locations are used solely for illustrative or contextual purposes. These references are **not endorsements or allegations**, nor are they intended to defame, criticize, or harm any entity or individual. Certain characters, names, and anecdotal examples may be fictionalized, composited, or altered to protect privacy and avoid identification, especially where personal stories or experiences are shared.

This book does not represent the views of any governmental agency, political organization, or corporate body. It is intended to raise awareness, foster dialogue, and encourage constructive action toward environmental resilience and sustainability in India.

**Readers are advised to independently verify any practices, solutions, or conclusions described in this book before acting upon them.**

The author and publisher disclaim all liability for any loss, damage, or legal action resulting from the use, interpretation, or implementation of any information contained in this work.

# References

1. Centre for Science and Environment. (2023). *State of India's Environment Report*. CSE India. https://www.cseindia.org

2. Central Pollution Control Board. (2023). *Annual reports on air and water quality*. CPCB. https://cpcb.nic.in

3. Global Forest Watch. (2023). *India: Forest loss and land use trends (2001–2023)*. https://www.globalforestwatch.org

4. India Meteorological Department. (2024). *Annual Climate Summary Reports*. IMD. https://mausam.imd.gov.in

5. International Pollutants Elimination Network. (2023). *Microplastics in human blood samples: India findings*. IPEN. https://ipen.org

6. IIT Kanpur & IIT Delhi. (2022). *Urban air pollution research publications. Atmospheric Environment, Nature Sustainability*. https://www.sciencedirect.com / https://www.nature.com

7. Ministry of Jal Shakti. (2023). *Aquifer depletion and water availability report*. Government of India. https://jalshakti-ddws.gov.in

8. National Disaster Management Authority. (2023). *National Heatwave Action Plan*. NDMA. https://ndma.gov.in

9. NASA Earth Observatory. (2023). *Satellite data on Indian monsoons, heatwaves, and deforestation*.

   https://earthobservatory.nasa.gov

10. NITI Aayog. (2023). *Composite Water Management Index (CWMI)*. https://niti.gov.in

11. TERI - The Energy and Resources Institute. (2022). *Urban sustainability and climate vulnerability papers*.

    https://www.teriin.org

12. The Lancet Planetary Health. (2020). *Health effects of air pollution in India*.

    https://www.thelancet.com/journals/lanplh

13. UNEP - United Nations Environment Programme. (2023). *India country profile on climate*. https://www.unep.org

14. UNICEF India. (2021). *Children's Climate Risk Index: India*. https://www.unicef.org/india

15. WHO - World Health Organization. (2023). *Ambient and household air pollution: India country data*.

    https://www.who.int/airpollution/data

16. Greenpeace India. (2022). *Plastic pollution and environmental impact reports*. https://www.greenpeace.org/india

17. AIIMS, Delhi. (2022). *Pesticide contamination and health studies*. All India Institute of Medical Sciences.

18. Down to Earth, The Hindu, The Indian Express, The Economic Times. (2021–2024). *Journalistic reporting on climate, pollution, water, and biodiversity*. [Various articles cited in-text]

# From Reading to Doing: Your Climate Action Roadmap

You've seen the storm.

You've felt the urgency.

But now comes the real question:

**What will you do with what you now know?**

This section isn't just for reading.

It's for **activating.**

## 1 : The Greenprint for My Life

Fill in your personal sustainability goals.

**In My Home:**

- ..........
- ..........
- ..........
- ..........
- ..........
- ..........
- ..........
- ..........

**At Work or Business:**

- ..........
- ..........
- ..........
- ..........
- ..........
- ..........
- ..........

### In My Society / Community:

- 
- 
- 
- 
- 
- 
- 
- 

### What's One Habit I Can Start Tomorrow?

- 
- 
- 
- 
- 
- 
- 
- 

## 2 : 30-Day Green Habit Challenge

Try one task a day - or make each week a theme.

### Week 1 – Water Warriors

☐ Installed tap aerators

☐ Turned off RO for a day

☐ Measured how many litres I use daily

### Week 2 – Plastic Detox

☐ Refused ALL single-use plastics for 3 days

☐ Switched to cloth bag, metal bottle, bamboo brush

☐ Did a "plastic audit" of my home waste

### Week 3 – Air & Energy Heroes

☐ Used public transport/carpool twice

☐ Reduced AC time by 30%

☐ Switched to LEDs or unplugged unused chargers

## Week 4 - Greener Together

☐ Talked to 5 people about the climate crisis

☐ Joined a local or digital green group

☐ Planted a tree or donated for reforestation

## Which task made you feel most powerful?

- ______________________________
- ______________________________
- ______________________________
- ______________________________
- ______________________________
- ______________________________

## 3 : Your Climate Story

Write your personal "mini-chapter" here.

Was there a moment that made you feel the climate crisis?
A water cut, a heatwave, a child coughing at night?

🕮 Tell your story here. Just like the ones you read in this book.

*Want to be featured? Share your story online with the hashtag*

*#My2035Story*

## 4 : The Climate Action Checklist

Tick off what you've already done - and set new goals.

✅ I have:

☐ Refused plastic water bottles

☐ Talked about climate with family/friends

☐ Used public transport or carpooled

☐ Planted at least one tree

☐ Reduced my AC or RO usage

☐ Donated to an environmental cause

☐ Supported a sustainable brand

☐ Signed a climate pledge

☐ Hosted or joined a cleanup / green event

☐ Reflected on my impact

### My Next Goal:

- ............................................................
- ............................................................
- ............................................................
- ............................................................
- ............................................................
- ............................................................

## 5 : Pledge Wall (For You & Your Family)

Get your family, friends, team, or school group to write or sign here:

"I commit to taking small but powerful actions to make Bharat 2035 a comeback story – not a collapse."

👤 Name & Date: ______________________

💬 Action I'll Take:

__________________________________________________

👤 Name & Date: ______________________

💬 Action I'll Take:

__________________________________________________

👤 Name & Date: ______________________

💬 Action I'll Take:

__________________________________________________

👤 Name & Date: ______________________

💬 Action I'll Take:

__________________________________________________

👤 Name & Date: ______________________

💬 Action I'll Take:

__________________________________________________

*Hang a photo of this pledge page at home or work. Inspire others to sign too.*

## 6 : Bonus Tools & Community Access

Scan the QR code below to:

- 📥 Download your printable 30-Day Challenge
- 🌍 Join the **Bharat Green Movement** online (ⓕ ⓘ - greeninkbymudit)
- 📷 Submit your action photos for a community gallery
- 📅 Register your society or city for the next Green Run

☞ You've read the warning.
☞ You've seen the data.
☞ Now it's your turn to rewrite the story.

**Welcome to the movement.**
Let's not wait for 2035 to regret what we didn't do.